NICKY EPSTEIN'S
Knitted Flowers

NICKY EPSTEIN'S
Knitted Flowers

PHOTOGRAPHY BY JENNIFER LEVY

sixth&spring books

EDITORIAL DIRECTOR
Trisha Malcolm

ART DIRECTOR
Chi Ling Moy

GRAPHIC DESIGNER
Sheena Paul

BOOK DIVISION MANAGER
Erica Smith

INSTRUCTIONS EDITOR
Samantha Henri

INSTRUCTIONS PROOFREADER
Nancy N. Henderson

PHOTOGRAPHY
Jennifer Levy

FASHION STYLIST
Michelle Debisette

PRODUCTION MANAGER
David Joinnides

PRESIDENT, SIXTH&SPRING BOOKS
Art Joinnides

An imprint of Sixth&Spring Books
233 Spring Street,
New York, New York 10013
sixthandspringbooks.com

Paperback Edition
First Printing 2010

Library of Congress Cataloging-in-Publication Data

Library of Congress Control Number: 2005929982

ISBN 10: 1-933027-94-0
ISBN 13: 978-1-933027-94-4

Manufactured in China

1 3 5 7 9 10 8 6 4 2

First Paperback Edition, 2010

DEDICATED TO MY MOST DEVOTED FANS

SOME PEOPLE SAY "STOP AND SMELL THE FLOWERS"... I SAY "STOP AND KNIT THE FLOWERS." MOTHER NATURE'S MOST BEAUTIFUL OFFSPRING COME IN AN INFINITE VARIETY OF COLORS AND SHAPES. THEY MAKE PEOPLE HAPPY AT JOYOUS TIMES AND COMFORT THEM AT SAD TIMES. I HAVE ALWAYS LOVED FLOWERS AND FREQUENTLY MAKE THEM A PART OF MY DESIGNS. THEY ENHANCE A GARMENT, MAKE IT HAPPY AND MORE BEAUTIFUL, AND WILL NEVER DIE. THEY CAN BE USED AS A SUBTLE ACCENT OR BE THE ENTIRE MOTIF OF A KNITTED PIECE.

INCLUDED IN INSTRUCTIONS ARE YARN SUGGESTIONS AND COLORS USED FOR THE SAMPLES. I ENCOURAGE YOU TO EXPERIMENT WITH A VARIETY OF YARNS AND COLORS. WE HAVE SO MANY INTERESTING YARNS TO CHOOSE FROM IN OUR MARKET TODAY, AS COMPONENTS TO CREATE A BEAUTIFUL BOUQUET, A CORSAGE, OR A WHOLE FIELD OF FLOWERS.

I HAVE ALWAYS WANTED TO CREATE A BOOK OF KNITTED FLOWERS, AND IT WAS A JOY WORKING IN MY BOTANICAL YARN GARDEN. COME ON IN AND KNIT THE FLOWERS—THEY WILL LAST FOREVER!

Nicky Epstein

 *Stitch Pattern Flowers*

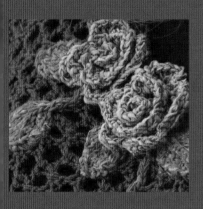

The following flowers are made with a variety of stitch patterns. The first few rows of a ruffle, twist, scallop, fringe or rib are worked to establish the outer edge of the flower. The final few rows are worked in decreases that shape the flower and form the center. The flowers can be layered, and stems and leaves may be added. Bobbles, bangles, buttons and beads sewn to the centers bring the flowers an extra touch of beauty. These flowers are quick and easy to make and can be used as adornments on anything you desire.

American Beauty Rose

MATERIALS

1 3OZ/85G SKEIN (EACH APPROX 122YD/110M) OF LION BRAND LION SUEDE (POLYESTER) IN #146 FUCHSIA

ONE PAIR SIZE 9 (5.5MM) NEEDLES

TAPESTRY NEEDLE

ROSE

CAST ON 66 STS.

WORK IN ST ST FOR 4 ROWS.

ROW 1 (RS) *K6, ROTATE LH NEEDLE COUNTERCLOCKWISE 360 DEGREES; REP FROM * TO END.

ROW 2 PURL.

ROW 3 K2TOG ACROSS—33 STS.

ROW 4 P2TOG TO LAST ST, P1— 17 STS.

ROW 5 K2TOG TO LAST ST, K1— 9 STS.

RUN THREADED TAPESTRY NEEDLE THROUGH REM STS ON NEEDLE, PULL TIGHTLY AND SECURE. TWIST ROSE INTO SPIRAL AND SEW BACK TO HOLD SPIRAL IN PLACE.

ROSEBUD

MATERIALS

1 3OZ/85G SKEIN (EACH APPROX 122YD/110M) OF LION BRAND LION SUEDE (POLYESTER) IN #140 ROSE

1 SKEIN IN #177 SAGE (B) FOR LEAVES

ONE PAIR SIZE 9 (5.5MM) NEEDLES

TAPESTRY NEEDLE

ROSEBUD

WITH A, CAST ON 42 STS.

WORK IN ST ST FOR 4 ROWS.

ROW 1 (RS) *K6, ROTATE LH NEEDLE COUNTERCLOCKWISE 360 DEGREES; REP FROM * TO END.

ROW 2 PURL.

ROW 3 K2TOG ACROSS—21 STS.

ROW 4 P2TOG TO LAST ST, P1— 11 STS.

ROW 5 K2TOG TO LAST ST, K1— 6 STS.

RUN THREADED TAPESTRY NEEDLE THROUGH REM STS ON NEEDLE, PULL TIGHTLY AND SECURE. TWIST ROSE INTO SPIRAL AND SEW BACK TO HOLD SPIRAL IN PLACE.

LEAF

(MAKE 4)

WITH B, MAKE 4 SMALL BASIC LEAVES (SEE PAGE 127) AND ATTACH TO FLOWERS.

Rose Pillow

Knitted Measurements

14"/35cm square

Materials

6 3oz/85g balls (each approx 122yd/110m of Lion Brand Lion Suede (polyester) in #146 fuchsia

One pair size 9 (5.5mm) needles or size to obtain gauge

14"/35cm square pillow form

Gauge

12 sts and 18 rows = 4"/10cm over St st using size 9 (5.5mm) needles.

Take time to check gauge.

Pillow Cover

Cast on 44 sts and work St st for 13¾"/34.5cm, ending with a RS row. K 3 rows. Cont in St st for 13¾"/34.5cm, more. Bind off.

Roses

(make 25)

Cast on 66 sts. Work in St st for 4 rows.

Next Row *K6, rotate the LH needle counterclockwise 360 degrees, then knit another 6 sts and rotate the LH needle again counterclockwise 360 degrees; rep from * to the end. P 1 row.

Next Row (RS) *K2 tog; rep from * to end—33 sts. Next row *P2 tog; rep from *, end P1—17 sts. Next row *K2 tog; rep from *, end K1—9 sts.

Cut yarn and thread through rem 9 sts, pull tightly. Twist to form a rose shape.

Finishing

Sew roses to one side of cover, 5 across and 5 down. Sew side and top seams. Insert pillow and sew remaining seam.

Twist Flower

MATERIALS

1 3oz/85g skein (each approx 122yd/110m) of Lion Brand Lion Suede (polyester) in #146 Fuchsia (A)

1 skein each in #140 Rose (B) and #177 Sage (C)

One pair size 9 (5.5mm) needles

Tapestry needle

FLOWER
(make 5)

With A, cast on 36 sts.

Rows 1–4 Work in garter st.
Row 5 (RS) *K6, rotate the LH needle counterclockwise 360 degrees; rep from * to end.
Row 6 K2tog across—18 sts.
Row 7 K2tog across—9 sts.

Row 8 K2tog to last st, k1—5 sts.
Run threaded tapestry needle through rem sts on needle, pull tightly and secure. Overlap last twist over first twist and sew in place.

BOBBLE
(make 5)

With B, make 5 bobbles (see page 127). Sew bobble to center of flower.

LEAF
(make 7)

With C, make 7 small basic leaves (see page 127) and attach to flowers.

Floral Clusters

MATERIALS

1 1¾oz/50g skein each (each approx 99yd/90m) of Muench String of Pearls (cotton/viscose/polyester) in assorted colors using 3 different colors for each flower, 1 color for small center, 1 color for larger outer flower, 1 color for French knots

One pair size 5 (3.75mm) needles

Tapestry needle

SMALL CENTER FLOWER

(make 9)

With 1st color, cast on 5 sts.

Row 1 K1f&b of each st—10 sts.

Rows 2 and 4 Purl.

Row 3 Rep row 1—20 sts.

Row 5 Bind off 1 st, *sl st from RH needle to LH needle, using cable cast on method, cast on 3 sts, bind off 5 sts; rep from * until 1 st rem. Fasten off.

LARGE OUTER FLOWER

(make 9)

With 2nd color, cast on 4 sts.

Row 1 K1f&b of each st—8 sts.

Rows 2, 4 and 8 Purl.

Row 3 Rep row 1—16 sts.

Row 5 Rep row 1—32 sts.

Row 7 Bind off 1 st, *sl st from RH needle to LH needle, using cable cast on method, cast on 3 sts, bind off 5 sts; rep from * until 1 st rem. Fasten off.

Gather cast on sts at center. Pull tightly and secure. Sew seams. Place center flower inside outer flower. Sew tog. With 3rd color, work three 3 French knots (see page 127) in each center.

Necklette

FLORAL SCARF

KNITTED FLORAL MEDALLIONS IN VARIOUS SIZES SEWN TOGETHER TO FORM A SCARF.

KNITTED MEASUREMENTS

APPROX 5" X 25"/12.5CM X 63.5CM

MATERIALS

1 1¾OZ/50G SPOOLS (EACH APPROX 143YD/130M) OF RUSSI SALES SERPENTINE (POLYAMIDE) EACH IN #929 GOLD, #841 DK GREEN AND #824 OLIVE

ONE PAIR SIZE 5 (3.75MM) NEEDLES OR SIZE TO OBTAIN GAUGE

TWO SIZE 3 (3.25MM) DPN FOR I-CORD BUTTON

GAUGES

1 FIVE PETAL FLOWER = 2"/5CM IN DIAMETER
1 SIX PETAL FLOWER = 2½"/6.5CM IN DIAMETER

1 SEVEN PETAL FLOWER = 3"/7.5CM IN DIAMETER

TAKE TIME TO CHECK GAUGES.

NOTE SCARF IS MADE UP OF THREE DIFFERENT SIZE FLOWERS: SMALL, MEDIUM AND LARGE. COLORS ARE CHANGED AS DESIRED.

FIVE PETAL FLOWER (SMALL)
(MAKE 5)
(MULTIPLE OF 11 STS PLUS 2)
CAST ON 57 STS
ROW 1 PURL.
ROW 2 K2, *K1, SL THIS ST BACK TO LEFT NEEDLE, LIFT THE NEXT 8 STS ON LEFT NEEDLE OVER THIS ST AND OFF NEEDLE, (YO) 2 TIMES, KNIT THE 1ST ST AGAIN, K2; REP FROM * TO END.
ROW 3 K1, *P2 TOG, DROP 1 YO LOOP ([K1, P1] 2 TIMES) IN REM YO OF PREVIOUS ROW, P1; REP FROM * TO LAST ST, K1. CHANGE TO A NEW COLOR.
ROW 4 KNIT.
ROW 5 *K2TOG; REP FROM * TO END.
ROW 6 *K2 TOG; REP FROM * TO END.
WITH TAPESTRY NEEDLE THREAD TAIL THROUGH REM 8 STS ON NEEDLE. GATHER UP AND FASTEN SECURELY. SEW SEAM AND WEAVE IN END.

SIX PETAL FLOWER (MEDIUM)
(MAKE 5)
(MULTIPLE OF 11 STS PLUS 2
CAST ON 68 STS.
ROWS 1–3 WORK AS FOR 5-PETAL FLOWER.
ROW 4 KNIT. CHANGE TO A NEW COLOR.
ROW 5, 6, 7, 8 KNIT. CHANGE TO A NEW COLOR.
ROW 9 K1, *K2TOG; REP FROM * TO LAST ST, K1.
ROW 10 K1, *K2 TOG; REP FROM * TO END.
ROW 11 *K2 TOG; REP FROM * TO END.
CUT YARN LEAVING 6"/15.5CM TAIL. WITH TAPESTRY NEEDLE THREAD TAIL THROUGH REM STS ON NEEDLE. GATHER UP AND FASTEN SECURELY. SEW SEAM AND WEAVE IN END.

SEVEN PETAL FLOWER (LARGE)
(MAKE 8)
MULTIPLE OF 11 STS PLUS 2
CAST ON 79 STS.
ROWS 1–3 WORK AS FOR 5-PETAL FLOWER. CHANGE TO A NEW COLOR.
ROWS 4, 5 AND 6 KNIT. CHANGE TO A NEW COLOR.
ROWS 7, 8, 9 KNIT. CHANGE TO A NEW COLOR.
ROWS 10, 11 KNIT. CHANGE TO A NEW COLOR.
ROW 12 K1 *K2 TOG; REP FROM * TO LAST ST, K1— 23 STS.
ROW 13 K1, *K2TOG; REP FROM * TO END—12 STS.
ROW 14 *K2 TOG; REP FROM * TO END—6 STS.
CUT YARN LEAVING 6"/15.5CM TAIL. WITH TAPESTRY NEEDLE THREAD TAIL THROUGH REM STS ON NEEDLE. GATHER UP AND FASTEN SECURELY. SEW SEAM AND WEAVE IN END.

CORD BUTTON
WITH DPN AND (C) CAST ON 4 STS. * K, SLIDE STS TO RIGHT END OF NEEDLE; REPEAT FROM * UNTIL 3" LONG. TIE OFF. TIE ONCE TO FORM A BUTTON KNOT. USE CAST ON AND BIND OFF TAIL TO TIE TO SCARF. LAY OUT FLOWERS AND STITCH TOGETHER WITH SEWING THREAD.

Buttercups

Materials

1 1¾oz/50g ball (each approx 137.5yd/125m) of Filatura Di Crosa 501 (wool) in Gold #503 (A)

Small amount contrasting color for French knot (B)

One pair size 3 (3.25mm) needles

Tapestry needle

7 Petals/French Knot Center

With A, cast on 43 sts.

Row 1 (RS) *K1, yo, k5, sl 2nd, 3rd, 4th and 5th sts over 1st st, yo; rep from * to last st, k1—29 sts. 7 petals.

Row 2 P1, *p3tog, p1; rep from * to end—15 sts.

Row 3 K1, *k2tog; rep from * to end—8 sts. Turn, pass 2nd, 3rd, 4th, 5th, 6th, 7th and 8th sts over 1st st. Fasten off.

Sew seam. With B, make a French knot (see page 127) in center of flower.

8 Petals/ French Knot Center

With A, cast on 42 sts.

Row 1 (RS) K1, yo, *k5, sl 2nd, 3rd, 4th, 5th st over 1st st, yo; rep from * to last st, k1—19 sts. 8 petals.

Row 2 P1, *p2tog—10 sts.

Row 3 K2tog across row—5 sts. Pass 2nd, 3rd, 4th, 5th st over first st. Fasten off.

Sew seam. With B, make a French knot (see page 127) in center of flower.

Bridal Gloves

MATERIALS

2 1¾oz/50g balls (each approx 55yd/51m) of Presencia Finca Perle Cotton SS12 (Egyptian cotton) in #3000 Off white

Small amount of sequins and 3mm pearls

One pair size 1 (2.25mm) needles

Small sewing needle and corresponding thread

Purchased pair of gloves

LES FLEURS

Make 8 small and 1 medium flower for each glove (see page 84).

LEAVES

Make 10 small basic leaves (see page 127) for each glove.

FINISHING

Place cardboard into glove. Pin flowers and leaves to the glove as shown in photo. With sewing needle, place a sequin and pearl into the center of each flower at the same time stitching it to the glove. Stitch around flowers and leaves to hold them in place.

Ruffle Rose

MATERIALS

1⅞oz/25g skein (each approx 137yd/125m) of Bouton d'Or Flash (viscose/polyamide) in #285 Jonquille (A)

1 skein in #447 Pottery (B), #053 Sapphire Blue (C) and #304 Lichen (D)

One pair size 5 (3.75mm) needles

Tapestry needle

FLOWER

(make 1 A, 1 B and 1 C)

Cast on 37 sts, leaving a long tail for seaming.

Row 1 K1, *p1, k1; rep from * to end.

Rows 2, 4, 6, 8 and 10 K the knits and p the purls.

Row 3 K1, *p1, m1-p, k1; rep from * to end—55 sts.

Row 5 K1, *p2, m1-p, k1; rep from * to end—73 sts.

Row 7 K1, *p3, m1-p, k1; rep from * to end—91 sts.

Row 9 K1, *p4, m1-p, k1; rep from * to end—109 sts.

Bind off all sts.

Roll the ruffle edge and seam the cast-on edge to form a rose shape.

LEAF

With D, make small basic leaves (see page 127) and attach.

Rose Bag

KNITTED MEASUREMENTS
Approx 7" x 5"/18cm x 12.5cm

MATERIALS
2 1¾oz/50g balls (each approx 167yd/ 155m) of Lang Opal (rayon/nylon) each in #26 sand (MC) and #94 ecru (CC)

One pair each sizes 2 and 4 (2.5 and 3.5mm) needles or size to obtain gauge

Two size 2 (2.5mm) dpn

Cable needle

8"/20.5cm of ½"/13mm wide ribbon

GAUGE
23 sts and 38 rows to 4"/10cm over St st using double strand and larger needles. Take time to check gauge.

ROSE
(make 17)

With smaller needles and single strand CC, cast on 37 sts.

Row 1 (RS) K1, *p1, k1; rep from * to end.

Rows 2, 4, 6, 8 and 10 K the knit and p the purl sts.

Row 3 K1, *p1, m1-p, k1; rep from * to end.

Row 5 K1, *p2, m1-p, k1; rep from * to end. Cont in this way to inc 18 sts every other row until there are 109 sts. Bind off. Roll ruffle edge from outside and sew along cast-on edge to form a rose.

Leaves

(make 17)

With smaller needles and single strand MC, cast on 15 sts.

Row 1 (RS) k6, sl2tog knitwise, k1, p2sso, (S2K1P), k6.

Row 2 k6, p1, k6.

Row 3 k5, S2K1P, k5.

Row 4 k5, p1, k5.

Row 5 k4, S2K1P, k4.

Row 6 k4, p1, k4.

Row 7 k3, S2K1P, k3.

Row 8 k3, p1, k3.

Row 9 k2, S2K1P, k2.

Row 10 k2, p1, k2.

Row 11 k1, S2K1P, k1.

Row 12 k1, p1, k1.

Row 13 S2K1P. Fasten off last st.

Bag Body

With larger needles and double strand MC, cast on 69 sts. Work in St st until piece measures 5½"/14cm. Change to smaller needles and single strand of MC and work in k1, p1 rib for ¾"/2cm. Then, work rows 3–9 of roses. Bind off in pat.

Bag Bottom

With RS facing, larger needles and double strand MC, pick up and k 70 sts evenly around cast-on edge of body. P 1 row on WS.

Row 1 *SK2P, k11; rep from * to end.

Row 2 and all WS rows Purl.

Row 3 *SK2P, k9; rep from * to end. Cont in this way to dec 10 sts every other row until 10 sts rem.

Row 13 K2tog across—5 sts. Cut yarn and thread through sts on needle. Draw up tightly and secure.

CABLED I-CORD DRAWSTRING

WITH 2 DPN AND SINGLE STRAND MC, CAST ON 5 STS. *ROW 1 K5. DO NOT TURN. SLIDE STS TO BEG OF NEEDLE TO WORK NEXT ROW FROM RS; REP FROM * 3 TIMES MORE. **ROW 5 (RS)** K1, SL 1 ST TO CN AND HOLD TO FRONT, K2, K1 FROM CN, K1. REP ROWS 1–5 FOR CABLED I-CORD UNTIL CORD MEASURES 34"/86CM. BIND OFF. MAKE A 2ND 8"/20.5CM CABLED I-CORD FOR STRAP.

FINISHING

BLOCK BAG TO MEASUREMENTS. FOLL PHOTO, SEW 15 ROSES AND 14 LEAVES TO BAG. SEW LOWER AND BACK SEAMS. USE RIBBON TO FORM A DRAWSTRING CASING AT INSIDE OF RIBBED EDGE. PULL DRAWSTRING THROUGH CASING AND SEW REM ROSES AND LEAVES TO CORD ENDS.

Fringe Loop Stitch Flower

SIZES

Small (Medium, Large)

MATERIALS

1 1¾oz/50g ball (each approx 75yd/71m) of Knit One, crochet too tartelette (cotton/tactel/nylon) in #519 Kaleidoscope

One pair size 8 (5mm) needles

Tapestry needle

Sewing thread

NOTE Novelty fur yarn or ribbon is suggested for this flower.

GARTER STITCH FRINGE

Cast on 4 sts. Work in garter st for 8 (12, 16)"/20.5 (30.5, 40.5)cm. Bind off 1 st, fasten off 2nd st. Sl rem 2 sts off needle and unravel them on every row.

Roll into a circle and sew in place.

Blossom

MATERIALS

1 3½oz/100g skein (each approx 165yd/150m) of Plymouth Eros Extreme (nylon) in #100 Multicolor

One pair size 10½ (6.5mm) needles

Beads for center

Tapestry needle

FLOWER

Cast on 30 sts.

Rows 1 & 3 (WS) K1 *make loop as folls: insert needle in st, wrap yarn over 2 fingers of LH 3 times, then over needle again—4 loops on needle. Draw 4 loops on needle through st, insert LH needle through the front loops and k them tog through back loops; rep from *, end k1.

Row 2 K1, k2tog across row—15 sts .

Row 4 K1, k2tog across row—8 sts. Pass 2nd, 3rd, 4th, 5th, 6th, 7th and 8th st over 1st st. Pull yarn through last loop and secure.

Sew seam. Center beads, bobbles and feathers are optional.

SMALL BLOSSOM FLOWER

Cast on 12 sts.

Row 1 (WS) K1, *make loop as foll: insert needle in st, wrap yarn over 2 fingers of LH 3 times, then over needle again—4 loops on needle. Draw 4 loops on needle through st, insert LH needle through the front loops and k them tog through back loops; rep from *, end k1.

Row 2 K2tog across row—6 sts. Pass 2nd, 3rd, 4th, 5th and 6th st over 1st st. Pull yarn through last loop and secure.

Sew seam. Fasten to center of blossom, or use separately.

Basic Flower

MATERIALS

A VARIETY OF YARN OF YOUR CHOOSING.

CORRESPONDING NEEDLE SIZES

TAPESTRY NEEDLE

FLOWER

CAST ON 6 STS.

ROWS 1–3 KNIT.

ROW 4 SL 1, K3, WITH LH NEEDLE LIFT 2ND, 3RD, AND 4TH STS OVER 1ST ST, K2—3 STS.

ROW 5 KNIT.

ROW 6 CAST ON 3 STS, K TO END—6 STS.

REP ROWS 1–6 FIVE MORE TIMES. BIND OFF.

RUN THREADED TAPESTRY NEEDLE THROUGH STRAIGHT EDGE OF PIECE. PULL TIGHTLY AND SECURE. SEW LAST BOUND-OFF EDGE TO CAST-ON EDGE FOR 3 STS STARTING AT CENTER.

NOTE CENTER OF FLOWER MAY BE LEFT OPEN TO SHOW HOLE (SEE PHOTO) OR PULLED TIGHTLY TO CLOSE HOLE. PETAL AMOUNT CAN BE CHANGED BY DOING MORE OR LESS REPS. EACH REP FORMS A PETAL.

Cardi Wrap

SIZE
ONE SIZE

KNITTED MEASUREMENTS
25¼"/64CM X 79"/200.5CM

MATERIALS
12 1¾OZ/50G SKEINS (EACH APPROX
108YD/98M) KARABELLA PIUMA
GOLD (KID MOHAIR/METALLIC/POLY-
ESTER) IN #6 CELERY

ONE PAIR SIZE 10 (6MM) NEEDLES
OR SIZE TO OBTAIN GAUGE

TAPESTRY NEEDLE

GAUGE
15 STS AND 19 ROWS = 4"/10 CM
OVER REVERSE ST ST.
TAKE TIME TO CHECK GAUGE.

NOTE SEE SCHEMATICS PAGE 131.

Wrap

Cast on 95 sts loosely. Work in reverse St st until piece measures 32"/81.5cm, ending with a WS row.

Left Armhole Shaping

*Next Row (RS) P37, bind off next 33 sts, p rem 25 sts.

Next Row (WS) K to bound off sts, cast on 33 sts, k to end *. Cont even in reverse St st for 15"/38cm., ending with a WS row.

Right Armhole Shaping

Rep from * to * for right armhole. Work even for 32"/81.5cm. Bind off loosely

Sleeves

Cast on 35 sts. Work in reverse St st inc 1 st each side every **6th row** 15 times—65 sts. Cont even until piece measures 20"/51cm. Bind off

Finishing

Sew sleeve seams. Sew sleeves into armholes

Scallops

Weave yarn in and out every 2 bars 8 times along bottom edges and center sleeve, gather and tie.

Flowers

(make 24)

Cast on 6 sts.

Rows 1–3 Knit.

Row 4 Sl 1, k3, with LH needle lift 2nd, 3rd, and 4th sts over first st, k2—3 sts

Row 5 Knit.

Row 6 Cast on 3 sts, k to end— 6 sts

Rep rows 1–6 five more times. Bind off

Run threaded tapestry needle through straight edge of piece. Pull tightly and secure.

Tie a flower to each gathered scallop, with open edges facing gathered sts, having 11 on each end of wrap and 1 on each sleeve. Sew around each flower to keep it in place.

Cabbage Rose

MATERIALS

1 1¾oz/50g skein (each approx 85yd/78m) of Berroco Cotton Twist (mercerized cotton/rayon) in #8314 Jonquil (A)

1 skein in #8372 Linoleum (B)

One pair each size 7 and 8 (4.5 and 5mm) needles

Tapestry needle

FLOWER

(make 5)

With A and size 7 needles, cast on 10 sts.

Row 1 (RS) Knit.

Row 2 and all even rows Purl.

Row 3 *K1f&b of st; rep from * to end—20 sts.

Row 5 * K1f&b of st; rep from* to end—40 sts.

Row 7 *K1f&b of st; rep from * to end—80 sts.

Row 8 Purl.

Bind off.

FLOWER SHAPING

To shape rose, twist to form spiral and sew in place at back.

LEAF

(make 8)

With 2 strands B held tog, make slip knot. With size 8 needles, cast on 5 sts, bind off 5 sts. Sl rem st to LH needle. Cast on 8 sts, bind off 8 sts. Fasten off rem st. Sew to flowers (see photo).

Passion Flower

MATERIAL

1 1¾OZ/50G SKEIN (EACH APPROX 68YD/61M) OF PRISM CHARMEUSE RIBBON (RAYON) IN LIPSTICK

ONE PAIR SIZE 9 (5.5MM)NEEDLES

POLKA DOT FEATHER CENTER FROM M & J; WWW.MJTRIM.COM

TAPESTRY NEEDLE

FLOWER

CAST ON 4 STS.

ROW 1 (WS) K1, YO, K1, YO, K2—6 STS.

ROWS 2 AND 4 KNIT.

ROW 3 K2, YO, K2TOG, YO, K2—7 STS.

ROW 5 K3, YO, K2TOG, YO, K2—8 STS.

ROW 6 BIND OFF 4 STS, K TO END—4 STS.

REP ROWS 1–6 SIX TIMES MORE.

RUN THREADED TAPESTRY NEEDLE THROUGH STRAIGHT EDGE OF PIECE, PULL TIGHTLY AND SECURE. SEW SEAM. SEW FEATHER TO CENTER.

Belt

SIZE

FITS WAIST SIZES
26"–30"(66CM–76CM)

MATERIALS

1 1¾OZ/50G BALL (EACH APPROX
120YD/110M) OF BERROCO SUEDE
(NYLON) IN #3714 HOPALONG
CASSIDY
ONE PAIR SIZE 9 (5.5MM) NEEDLES
LARGE TAPESTRY NEEDLE
5 CORRESPONDING BEADS
5 FEATHERS
1¼" X 67"/170CM SUEDE
MATTE KNIFE AND STRAIGHT EDGE
20 GROMMETS AND FASTENERS

NOTE FLOWERS CAN BE ADDED TO
PURCHASED BELT.

PASSION FLOWER

HOLDING 2 STRANDS OF SUEDE
YARN TOG, MAKE 5 PASSION FLOW-
ERS (SEE PAGE 44).

PISTIL FLOWER

HOLDING 2 STRANDS OF SUEDE
YARN TOG, MAKE 5 PISTILS (SEE
PAGE 102).

PLACE PISTIL FLOWER IN CENTER
OF PASSION FLOWER AND SEW TOG.
SEW A BEAD TO CENTER OF
FLOWER. GLUE FEATHERS TO BOT-
TOM OF EACH FLOWER.

BELT

CUT PIECES OF LEATHER AS FOLL:
2 PIECES 1¾"/4.5CM WIDE X 20½"/
52CM LONG FOR FRONT PIECES.
4 PIECES 1¾"/4.5CM WIDE X 6½"/
16.5CM LONG FOR BACK PIECES.
ON EACH OF THE 2 FRONT PIECES,
FOLD 1 END OVER ½"/1.25CM AND
APPLY 1 GROMMET AT EACH CORNER
OF FOLDED PIECE.
ON EACH OF THE 4 BACK PIECES,
FOLD EACH END OVER ½"/1.25CM
AND APPLY 1 GROMMET AT EACH

CORNER OF EACH FOLDED PIECE.
CUT OUT 4 HORIZONTAL SECTIONS
OF SUEDE (SAVING PIECES)
⅛"/.37CM WIDE X 5"/12.5CM LONG
EVENLY SPACED ALONG EACH OF
4 BACK PIECES BEGINNING AND
ENDING WITHIN ½"/1.25CM OF
GROMMET END.
JOIN THE 4 BACK SECTIONS OF
BELT WITH METAL FASTENERS
THROUGH EACH GROMMET, THEN
JOIN FRONT PIECES AT EACH END
IN SAME MANNER.
ON 2 FRONT PIECES, CUT INTO 8
EQUAL STRIPS FOR FRINGE START-
ING ½" FROM GROMMET EDGE TO
END OF PIECE.
USING SCRAP PIECES OF SUEDE
CUT FROM BACK SECTIONS, ATTACH
5 FLOWERS AT EACH SECTION
JOINING.

 *Florets*

MATERIALS

SMALL AMOUNTS 1¾OZ/50G
SKEIN (EACH APPROX
137.5YD/125M) OF FILATURA DI
CROSA 501 (WOOL) IN VARIETY OF
COLORS

ONE PAIR SIZE 5 (3.75MM) NEEDLES

TAPESTRY NEEDLE

FLOWER

(MAKE 13 ASSORTED COLORS)
CAST ON 21 STS LOOSELY. WORK 3
ROWS IN GARTER ST. PASS ALL STS
ONE AT A TIME OVER 1ST ST AND
FASTEN OFF.

TURN CAST-ON EDGE INTO BOUND-
OFF EDGE MAKING ONE TWIST TO
SHAPE FLORETTE. SEW IN PLACE.

Ramonda

SIZES SMALL (MEDIUM, LARGE)

MATERIALS

1 1¾OZ/50G BALL (EACH APPROX
121YD/110M) OF MUENCH YARNS
MYSTIK (COTTON) IN #51 LIGHT
PEACH

1 BALL EACH IN #82 PEACH, #91
SALMON, AND #50 BURGUNDY FOR
FLOWERS

ONE PAIR SIZE 5 (3.75MM) NEEDLES

TAPESTRY NEEDLE

FLOWER

USING 2 COLORS FOR EACH
FLOWER, WITH 1ST COLOR CAST ON
37 (43, 49) STS.

K 2 ROWS.

ROW 1 (RS) K1, *YO, K1, K3TOG,
K1, YO, K1; REP FROM *.

ROW 2 P1, *K5, P1; REP FROM *.
REP ROWS 1 & 2, 1 (2, 3) TIMES
MORE. CHANGE TO 2ND COLOR.

NEXT ROW K2TOG ACROSS, END
K1—19 (23, 25) STS.

NEXT ROW K2TOG ACROSS ROW.
FASTEN OFF.

SEW SEAMS.

Lady's Lace Flower

SIZES

Small (Large)

MATERIALS

1 1¾oz/50g skein (each approx 146yd/133m) of Blue Sky Alpaca & Silk (alpaca/silk) in #133 Pale Pink

one pair each size 3 and 5 (3.25 and 3.75mm) needles

Beads (optional)

Tapestry needle

FLOWERS

Cast on 49 sts for small or large flower.

Row 1 (WS) purl.

Row 2 k1, *yo, k1, sk2p, k1, yo, k1; rep from *.

Rep rows 1 and 2, 2 (3) times more.

Next Row purl.

Next Row p2tog across row, end p1—25 sts.

Next Row k2tog across row, end k1—13 sts.

run threaded tapestry needle run through rem sts. Pull tightly and fasten. sew seam. Sew beads to center.

Picot Flowers

SIZES

SMALL (LARGE)

MATERIALS

1 1¾OZ/50G SKEIN (EACH APPROX 123YD/112M) OF JCA SAUCY SPORT (COTTON) IN #370 ASHES OF ROSES

1 SKEIN EACH IN #138 IRIS AND #640 PURPLE PASSION

ONE PAIR SIZE 5 (3.75MM) NEEDLES

TAPESTRY NEEDLE

M & J CRYSTAL BUTTONS (OPTIONAL)

NOTE EACH BALL MAKES SEVERAL FLOWERS TO USE ON ITEMS OF YOUR CHOICE.

FLOWER

(USE 1 COLOR FOR EACH FLOWER)

CAST ON 17 STS FOR SMALL OR LARGE FLOWER.

ROW 1 KNIT.

ROW 2 BIND OFF 1 ST, * SL ST BACK TO LH NEEDLE, (USING CABLE CAST ON METHOD [SEE PAGE 128], CAST ON 2 STS, BIND OFF NEXT 2 STS, SL ST BACK TO LH NEEDLE) 3 (4) TIMES, USING CABLE CAST ON METHOD, CAST ON 2 STS, BIND OFF 6 STS; REP FROM * TO END.

RUN THREADED TAPESTRY NEEDLE THROUGH LOOP CAST ON EDGE, PULL TIGHTLY AND SECURE. SEW CRYSTAL BUTTON IN CENTER OF FLOWER, IF DESIRED (NOT SHOWN IN PHOTO).

Stellata Thistle

5 VERSIONS

MATERIALS

1 1¾oz/50g ball (each approx 138yd/126m) of alchemy Silk Purse (silk) in #82W Janbay Sapphire (A)

1 ball #02W Deep Sea (B)

One pair size 5 (3.75m) needles

Tapestry needle

Small amount of poly-fil

NOTE Make center ball for all versions and attach to the center of different flowers.

FLOWER

With B, cast on 8 sts leaving a long tail for seaming.

Row 1 *K1F&B in every st—16 sts.

Row 2 and all even rows Purl.

Rows 3, 5, 7 and 9 Knit.

Row 11 K2tog across row—8 sts.

run threaded tapestry needle through 8 sts. Pull tightly and secure. Thread cast on tail and loop through cast on sts and gather securing thread. Stuff with poly-fil. Sew side edges tog.

VERSION I

With 2 strands of A held tog, work as for pistil flower (see page 102) as foll:

First layer: Cast on and bind off 6 sts instead of 5 and work 9 reps.

Second layer: Cast on and bind off 9 sts instead of 5 and work 12 reps.

Place first layer on top of second layer and sew ball to center.

VERSION II

With A, work picot flower (see page 54). Sew ball to center .

VERSION III

Using 2 strands of yarn, work same as medium les fleurs (see page 84). Sew ball to center.

VERSION IV

With A, make medium size ramonda, (see page 50). Sew ball to center.

VERSION V

With A, make basic flower (see page 36). Sew ball to center.

Scallop Rose

MATERIALS

A VARIETY OF YARNS, INCLUDING
ANGORA, METALLIC TWEED, AND
WOOL.

ONE PAIR NEEDLES IN SIZE
CORRESPONDING TO YARN

TAPESTRY NEEDLE

ROSE

CAST ON 101 STS.

Row 1 (WS) PURL.

Row 2 K2, *K1 AND SL BACK TO
LH NEEDLE, WITH RH NEEDLE,
LIFT NEXT 8 STS, 1 ST AT A TIME
OVER THIS ST AND OFF NEEDLE,
YO TWICE, K FIRST ST AGAIN, K2;
REP FROM * TO END.

Row 3 P1, *P2 TOG, DROP FIRST
YO OF PREVIOUS ROW, K INTO
FRONT, BACK, FRONT, BACK AND
FRONT AGAIN IN 2ND YO = 5 STS,
P1; REP FROM *, END P1.

Row 4 KNIT.

BIND OFF KWISE.

TO SHAPE FLOWER, ROLL BO EDGE
TO FORM SPIRAL AND SEW IN
PLACE. FELT (SEE PAGE 128) IF
DESIRED.

Floral Ponchette with Beaded Edging

SIZE

ONE SIZE

MATERIALS

5 1¾OZ/50G SKEINS (EACH APPROX 100YD/92M) OF BERROCO SOFTWIST (RAYON/WOOL) #9420 NOVEAU BERRY (A)

1 1¾OZ/50G SKEIN (EACH APPROX 110YD/102M) OF BERROCO ZEN (NYLON/COTTON) IN #8228 DHARMA (B)

1 1¾OZ/50G SKEIN (EACH APPROX 110YD/102M) OF BERROCO ZEN COLOR IN #8026 NORI (C)

ONE PAIR SIZE 9 (5.5MM) OR SIZE TO OBTAIN GAUGE

SET DOUBLE-POINTED NEEDLES IN SIZE 7 (4.5MM)

BEADS—2⅛ YDS BEAD FRINGE FROM M&J; WWW.MJTRIM.COM

GAUGE

15 STS AND 18 ROWS = 4"/10CM IN PAT ST.
TAKE TIME TO CHECK GAUGE.

PATTERN STITCH (MULTIPLE OF 3 STS PLUS 4)
Row 1 (RS) K2, *SK2P, (YO) TWICE; REP FROM *, END K2.
Row 2 K2, *(P1, K1) INTO YO TWICE OF ROW 1, P1; REP FROM *, END K2.
Row 3 KNIT.
REP ROWS 1–3 FOR PAT.

PONCHO

RECTANGLE (MAKE 2)
CAST ON 55 STS. KNIT 4 ROWS.
WORK 56 REPS OF PAT. KNIT 3
ROWS. BIND OFF.

FINISHING

BLOCK EACH RECTANGLE TO MEAS-
URE 15 X 26" (38 X 66 CM). SEW
CAST-ON EDGE OF 1ST PIECE TO
RIGHT LOWER SIDE OF 2ND PIECE.
SEW BOUND-OFF EDGE OF 2ND
PIECE TO RIGHT LOWER EDGE OF
1ST PIECE LEAVING AN OPENING
FOR THE HEAD (SEE SCHEMATIC
PAGE 131, SEWING A TO A AND B
TO B).

ROSE

(MAKE 3)
WITH SIZE 9 NEEDLES AND B,
CAST ON 90 STS.
ROW 1 (WS) PURL.

ROW 2 K2, *K1 AND SL BACK TO
LH NEEDLE, WITH RH NEEDLE,
LIFT NEXT 8 STS, 1 ST AT A TIME,
OVER THIS ST AND OFF NEEDLE,
YO TWICE, K THE FIRST ST AGAIN,
K2; REP FROM * TO END.
ROW 3 P1, *P2TOG, DROP FIRST
YO OF PREVIOUS ROW, K INTO
FRONT, BACK, FRONT, BACK AND
FRONT AGAIN IN 2ND YO = 5 STS,
P1; REP FROM*, END P1.
ROW 4 KNIT.
ROW 5 BIND OFF KWISE.

TO SHAPE FLOWER, ROLL BOUND-
OFF EDGE TO FORM SPIRAL AND
SEW IN PLACE.

LEAVES

WITH DPNS AND C, CAST ON 3 STS.
ROW 1 K1,YO, K1,YO, K1—5 STS.
ROW 2 AND ALL EVEN-NUMBERED
ROWS PURL.

Row 3 K2, YO, K1, YO, K2—7 STS.
Row 5 K3, YO, K1, YO, K3—9STS.
Row 7 SSK, K5, K2TOG—7STS.
Row 9 SSK, K3, K2TOG—5STS.
Row 11 SSK, K1, K2TOG—3 STS.
Row 13 SK2P—1 ST. FASTEN OFF.

LEAVES WITH STEMS

CORD WITH DPNS AND C, CAST ON 3 STS. K3, DO NOT TURN WORK, SLIDE STS TO RIGHT SIDE OF NEEDLE, REP FROM* FOR SPECIFIED LENGTH OF CORD.

MAKE 3 LEAVES WITH 4" CORD, 2 WITH 3" CORD AND 4 WITH 1" CORD. WHEN CORD IS DESIRED LENGTH, WORK ROWS 1–13 OF LEAF PAT.

SEW ROSES AND LEAVES TO NECK FOLL PHOTO. SEW BEADS AROUND BOTTOM EDGE OF PONCHETTE.

Tea Rose

ROSE PILLOW

MATERIALS

1 .85oz/25g skein (each approx 151yd/138m) of Muench Soft Kid (super kid mohair/ nylon/wool) in #56 Rust (A)

1 skein in #64 Forrest (B)

One pair size 8 (5mm) needles

Tapestry needle

1 pin back

FLOWER

With A, cast 71 sts on loosely. Work 10 rows in reverse St st. Bind off 4 sts at beg of next 2 rows, 6 sts at beg of next 4 rows—39 sts.

Next Row (RS) K2tog across row, end k1—20 sts. Bind off. With WS facing center, roll bound-off edge, twist into a spiral to form rose and sew in place at back.

DOUBLE LEAVES

(make 2)

With B, make 2 large basic leaves (see page 127) and sew them tog making 1.

Sew 2 sets of double leaves to rose (see photo). Sew pin back to back of rose

CHAPTER TWO

Petal Constructed Flowers

THE WORD "CONSTRUCTED" SUITS THESE FLOWERS. INDIVIDUAL COMPONENTS (OR PIECES) SUCH AS PETALS, CORKSCREWS, BOBBLES AND FRINGES ARE KNIT OR SEWN TOGETHER TO SHAPE THE FLOWERS. YOU'LL FIND A VARIETY OF VERY SPECIAL, EASY-TO-LEARN TECHNIQUES IN THIS CHAPTER AND CAN CREATE A VARIETY OF BEAUTIFUL FLOWERS. EXPERIMENT WITH DIFFERENT TEXTURAL YARNS AND COLOR COMBINATIONS.

Wallflower

MATERIALS

1 .85oz/25g ball (each approx 225yd/205m) of Knit One, Crochet Too Douceur Et Soie (baby mohair/silk) in #8501 Soft Seafoam

1 ball in #8644 Soft Sky Blue

One pair each sizes 2 and 3 (2.5 and 3.25mm) needles

One 4mm or 6mm pearl for each flower

Tapestry needle

NOTE Both flowers are knit with same instructions, using 1 strand or size 2 (2.5mm) needles or 2 strands and size 3 (3mm) needles. Make 4 petals for each flower.

FLOWER

(make 4 petals)
Cast on 3 sts. With separate ball of yarn, cast on 3 sts on same needle—6 sts.
Row 1 RS * [K1, cast on 1] twice, K1; rep from * on 2nd set of sts with 2nd ball of yarn—5 sts each set.
Row 2 Purl.
Row 3 *K1, cast on 1, K3, cast on 1, K1; rep from * on 2nd set of sts—7 sts each set.
Row 4 Join the 2 sets of sts as foll: P6, p2tog, P6—13 sts.
Row 5 *K1, cast on 1, K11, cast on 1, K1—15 sts.
Rows 6, 8, 10, 12 and 14 Purl.
Row 7 K6, s2kp, K6—13 sts.
Row 9 K5, s2kp, K5—11 sts.
Row 11 Ssk, K2, s2kp, K2, k2tog—7 sts.
Row 13 Ssk, s2kp, k2tog—3 sts.
Leave sts on needle. Cont on free needle and make 3 more petals—12 sts on needle. P 1 row connecting 4 petals.

Run threaded tapestry needle through rem sts on needle, pull tightly and secure. Sew pearl to center.

Flower-Trimmed Cardigan

MATERIALS

1 .85OZ/25G BALL (EACH APPROX 225YD/205M) KNIT ONE, CROCHET TOO DOUCEUR ET SOIE (BABY MOHAIR/SILK) IN #8501 SOFT SEAFOAM

1 BALL IN #8644 SOFT SKY BLUE

ONE PAIR SIZE 3 (2.5MM) NEEDLES

ONE 4MM OR 6MM PEARL FOR EACH FLOWER

TAPESTRY NEEDLE

PURCHASED CARDIGAN

FLOWERS

USING SIZE 3 NEEDLES AND 2 STRANDS OF YARN HELD TOG, MAKE 18 WALLFLOWERS (SEE PAGE 68).

NOTE NUMBER OF FLOWERS MAY VARY DEPENDING ON PIECE YOU HAVE PURCHASED.

FINISHING

SEW 18 FLOWERS EVENLY SPACED AROUND ENTIRE OUTER EDGE OF CARDIGAN.

Corkscrew Flowers

CURLY Q

MATERIALS

1 1¾oz/50g skein (each approx 175yd/165m) of Koigu Painter's Palette premium Merino (Merino wool) in #P200 Blue/Pink

1 skein in # P444 Blue

One pair size 3 (3.25mm) needles

Tapestry needle

Beads: "And the beads go on" at www.Fireflybeads.com

CORKSCREW (right)

Cast on 60 sts over 2 needles.

Row 1 K1f&b of each st across

Row 2 Bind off pwise.

Use fingers to twist each tassel into 13 corkscrews. Weave in ends.

With spare needle, pick up 1 st on each of 13 twists—13 sts.

With separate needle cast on

52 sts. With both needles parallel, using a 3rd needle, k1,*k corkscrew and cast on st tog, k 3 cast on sts; rep from *, end k1—52 sts. K 3 rows.

Next Row K2, *k2tog, k2; rep from *, end k2—40 sts.

Next row K2tog across row—20 sts.

Next Row K2tog across row—10 sts.

Next row K2tog across—5 sts.

Bind off.

Sew seam, sew bead to center.

CANTERBURY (left)

Cast on 40 sts. Make 1 corkscrew. With spare needle, pick up 1 st on each twist—10 sts.

With separate needle, cast on

22 sts. With both needles parallel, using a 3rd needle, k1, *k corkscrew and cast-on st tog, k1 cast-on st; rep from *, end k1—22 sts.

Next Row Knit.

Next Row Purl.

Cont in reverse St st for 1"/2.5cm. Work in k1, p1 rib for ½"/1.25cm.

Next Row (WS) *k3tog, p3tog; rep from * end, k3tog, p1—8 sts.

(RS) K2tog across row—4 sts.

Change to dpns and work i-cord (see page 127) for desired length for stem.

Sew seam. Use purchased fringe beads or thread beads (see photo). Sew to center.

Corkscrew Flowers

CRAZY DAISY (LEFT)

MAKE 5 CORKSCREWS OF 40 CAST-ON STS EACH. WEAVE IN ENDS. TWIST TO SHAPE.

WITH A SPARE NEEDLE, PICK UP 2 STS AT EACH END OF EACH CORKSCREW (20 STS ON SAME NEEDLE.). ON SAME NEEDLE, CAST ON 1 ST AND K IT, *K4 (CORKSCREW STS), CAST ON 1 ST; REP FROM *—26 STS. K 3 ROWS.

NEXT ROW K1, K2TOG ACROSS ROW, END K1—14 STS.

REP LAST ROW—8 STS. PASS 2ND, 3RD, 4TH, 5TH, 6TH, 7TH AND 8TH ST OVER 1ST ST. PULL YARN THROUGH LAST LOOP AND SECURE. SEW SEAM. SEW ROUND BEAD IN CENTER.

PINWHEEL (RIGHT)

MAKE 7 CORKSCREWS OF 19 CAST-ON STS EACH. DO NOT FASTEN OFF. LEAVE CORKSCREWS ON SPARE NEEDLE. CAST ON 23 STS, *K2, K NEXT CAST ON ST WITH 1 CORKSCREW; REP FROM *, END K2—23 STS. K 4 ROWS.

NEXT ROW K1, K2TOG ACROSS ROW—12 STS.

NEXT ROW K2TOG ACROSS ROW—6 STS. PASS 2ND, 3RD, 4TH, 5TH AND 6TH ST OVER 1ST ST. PULL YARN THROUGH LAST LOOP AND SECURE.

SEW IN 6 BUGLE BEADS FOR CENTER.

Pop Daisy

MATERIALS

1 1¾oz/50g skein (each approx 165yd/150m) of Koigu Merino Wool (Merino wool) in #2250 Hot Pink

1 skein each in #1013 Lavender, #1000 Blue, #2132 Lime, #2200 Orange, #2100 Gold

One pair size 6 (4.25mm) needles

Tapestry needle

POP DAISY SINGLE COLOR PETALS (5 petals with same color)

*Cast on 6 sts.

Row 1 Knit.

Rows 2–5 Inc 1 st at beg of each row—10 sts.

Rows 6–14 Knit.

Rows 15–20 K2tog at beg of next 6 rows—4 sts.

Leave sts on needle. On same needle; rep from * 4 times more—20 sts.**

*Cast on 1 st and k it, k 4 sts from needle (1 petal); rep from *, end cast on 1 st — 26 sts.

K 2 rows.

Next Row K 1, k2tog across row, end k 1—14 sts.

Rep last row—8 sts. Pass 2nd, 3rd, 4th, 5th, 6th, 7th and 8th st over 1st st. Pull yarn through last loop and secure. Weave in ends.

CENTER

With a contrasting color, cast on 4 sts.

Row 1 Knit.

Rows 2–5 Inc 1 st at beg of next 4 rows—8 sts.

Rows 6–11 Knit.

Rows 12–15 K2tog at beg of next 4 rows—4 sts.

Bind off. Sew to center of flower.

POP DAISY MULTICOLOR PETALS

(make 5)

Make as for pop daisy changing color for each of 5 petals. Work petal only as for pop daisy to **, ending with 20 sts on needle. With new color, cast on 1 st and k it, k 20 sts, cast on 1 st—22 sts.

K 2 rows.

Next Row K1, k2tog across row, end k1—12 sts.

Next Row K2tog across row— 6 sts. Pass 2nd, 3rd, 4th, 5th and 6th st over 1st st. Pull yarn through last loop and secure. Weave in ends.

CENTER

Work as for pop daisy center.

Mod Podge Flora

MATERIALS

1 1¾oz/50g skein (each approx 176yd/160m) of Lana Grossa Merino 2000 (fine Merino wool) in #470 Orange (A)

1 skein each in #466 Blue (B), #481 Green (C) and # 433 Black (D)

One pair size 6 (4.25mm) needles

Size 5 double-pointed needles

Tapestry needle

NOTE Beg with 5 sts and end with multiple of 10 sts. Each petal is worked separately then all petals are joined on the same row. Cut yarn on all but last petal and leave sts on needle. Alternate colors A, B and C, maintaining Black (D) for center.

PETALS

(MAKE 5)

With A, cast on 5 sts. Work in garter st for 2"/5cm. Cut yarn and leave sts on needle. On same needle, cast on and work as before to make another strip. Cont in this manner until 5 strips are made—each strip makes 10 sts. To join petals on RS, with D cast on 1 st and k it, *k5, with RS facing, k5 from cast on edge; rep from * to last strip, cast on 1 st—52 sts.

NEXT ROW (WS) K1, k2 tog to last st, k1—27 sts. Change to C. K 2 rows. Change to D.

NEXT ROW (RS) K1, k2tog across row to last 2 sts, k2—15 sts.

NEXT ROW Knit. Change to B.

NEXT ROW (RS) K1, *sl 1, k 3; rep from *, end sl 1, k1.

NEXT ROW P1, *sl 1, p3; rep from * end sl 1, p1.

NEXT ROW (RS) Rep previous RS row.

NEXT ROW P2tog across row, end p1—8 sts. Pass 2nd, 3rd, 4th, 5th, 6th, 7th and 8th st over 1st st. Pull yarn through last loop and secure. Sew seam.

STEM

With dpns and C, cast on 3 sts. Work cord (see page 127) for desired length and attach.

Electra Floral

MATERIALS

1 1¾oz/50g ball (each 140yd/128m) of Muench Yarns Fonty Serpentine (polyamide) in #837 Hot Pink (A)

1 ball each in #848 Wine (B) and #918 Chartreuse (C)

One pair size 3 (3.25mm) needles

Tapestry needle

Beads (optional)

FLOWER

With A, cast on 4 sts.

Row 1 (RS) [K1, M1] 3 times, k1—7 sts

Row 2 and all even rows Purl.

Row 3 [K1, M1] 6 times, k1—13 sts.

Rows 5 and 7 Knit.

Row 9 K5, s2kp, k5—11 sts.

Row 11 K4, s2kp, k4—9 sts.

Row 13 K3, s2kp, k3—7 sts.

Row 15 K2, s2kp, k2—5 sts.

Row 16 Purl. Leave 5 sts on needle.

With free needle, rep rows 1–16 five more times, ending with row 15 on last rep—30 sts. Change to B.

Row 16 P4, *p2tog, p3; rep from *, end p2tog, p4—25 sts.

Rows 17 and 19 Knit.

Row 18 P2tog across row, end p1—13 sts.

Row 20 P2tog across row, end p1—7 sts. Pass 2nd, 3rd, 4th, 5th, 6th and 7th sts over 1st st. Fasten off last st connecting center, sew seam. Work in all ends. Sew beads to center (optional).

STEM

With dpns and C, cast on 3 sts. Work I-cord (see page 127) for desired length and sew to flower.

LEAF

With C, make one large garter stitch leaf (see page 127) and attach to stem.

CHAPTER THREE

Cord Flowers

Traditional I-Cord or knit cord is used to make a simple looped daisy and a variety of other flowers. The cord can be felted and folded to make loopy flowers, or wire can be used to bend and shape the petals. Casting on and binding off is another technique used to make cute, quick and easy flowers. These knitted flowers are perfect for adorning a holiday gift package, shoes, bags or anything you want to make special.

Les Fleurs

SIZES
Small (Medium, Large)

MATERIALS
Small amounts of Classic Elite Provence (mercerized cotton) in #2625 Rosa Rugosa (A) and #2601 Bleach (B) for 1 flower

Small amounts of Classic Elite LaGran (mohair/wool/nylon) in #6571 Julia's Pink (A) and #6554 French Lilac (B) for 1 flower

Small amounts of Classic Elite Temptation (silk) in #HAG1-27 Pastel Pink (A) and #HAG1-01white (B) for 1 flower

Small amounts of Classic Elite Beatrice (100% merino wool) in #3528 Rosso di Roma (A) and #3206 Marble (B) for 1 flower

One pair knitting needles in size corresponding to yarn used

Tapestry needle

FLOWER

VERSION 1
With A, cast on 35 (50, 65) sts.
Row 1 (RS) *with B, k1, bind off 5 (8, 11) sts (2 sts on RH needle); rep from * to end—10 sts.
Run threaded tapestry needle through rem sts on needle, pull tightly and secure.

VERSION 2
With A, cast on 35 (50, 65) sts.
Rows 1—4 Knit.
Row 5 Rep Row 1 of Version 1.
Run threaded tapestry needle through rem sts on needle, pull tightly and secure.

Felted Cord Flowers

SWEETHEART FLOWER

MATERIALS

1 ⅞oz/25g skein (each approx 82yd/ 75m) of Jamieson Shetland Double Knitting (pure Shetland wool) in #555 Light Pink (A)

1 skein in #575 Lipstick (B)

1 skein in #580 Cherry (C)

1 skein in #595 Maroon (D)

1 skein in #525 Crimson (E)

Set size 8 (5mm) double-pointed needles

Seven 6"/15cm long pieces of thin wire

Tapestry needle

SWEETHEARTS

With E, work cord 56"/142 cm long. Felt cord (see page 128). Cut seven 6"/15cm lengths. Run wire through cord, fold each into heart shape. Sew 4 hearts tog at bottom points. Sew 3 hearts in the same way. Place the 3 hearts on top of the 4 hearts and stitch tog. With E, make 1 bobble (see page 127), felt and tie to center.

Cord Blooms

LAYERED FLOWER, CORD DAISY, AND CORD BLOSSOM

LAYERED FLOWER (BACK) WITH A, WORK 16"/40.5CM I-CORD (SEE PAGE 127). WITH B, WORK 24"/61CM CORD. WITH C, WORK 34"/86CM CORD. WITH D, MAKE BOBBLE (SEE PAGE 127). FELT (SEE PAGE 128) CORDS AND BOBBLE.

HINT WHEN FELTING CORD, PLACE A RUBBER BAND LOOSELY AROUND FOLDED CORD TO KEEP IT FROM TANGLING.

TOP LAYER: FOLD A CORD INTO FIVE 1"/2.5CM LONG ACCORDION LOOPS HOLDING THEM IN PLACE WITH SCOTCH TAPE. THREAD NEEDLE AND RUN THROUGH THE ROUND EDGE OF LOOPS. GATHER AND TIE TO SHAPE FLOWER.

2ND AND 3RD LAYERS: REP TOP LAYER AS FOLL: WITH B CORD, FOLD INTO SEVEN 1½"/4CM LOOPS. WITH C CORD, FOLD INTO NINE 1¾"/4.5CM LOOPS. WORK AS FOR TOP LAYER TO FORM FLOWER. PLACE FLOWERS IN LAYERS AND STITCH TOG. TIE BOBBLE TO CENTER.

CORD DAISY (LEFT) WORK SAME AS LAYERED FLOWER, USING 1 CORD OF A ONLY FOR FLOWER. WITH B, MAKE 1 TO 3 BOBBLES AND PLACE IN CENTER.

CORD BLOSSOM (FRONT) WORK SAME AS LAYERED FLOWER, WORKING CORDS AS FOLL: WITH D, WORK CORD 96"/244CM LONG. FELT CORD (SEE PAGE 128).

STEM MAKE TWO 6"/15CM CORDS WITH B, ONE 7"/18CM CORD WITH D. FELT CORD (SEE PAGE 128). FOLD CORD D INTO SIXTEEN 2"/5CM LOOPS. THREAD TAPESTRY NEEDLE AND GATHER SAME AS LAYERED FLOWER, PULL TIGHTLY AND SECURE.

WITH B, MAKE 3 BOBBLES, FELT AND TIE TO CENTER. ATTACH STEMS TO BACK OF FLOWER, CUT AT ANGLES. HINT: WHEN FOLDING CORD, USE LINE PAPER OR DRAW 2 LINES TO USE AS A TEMPLATE FOR FOLDING CORD TO SIZE.

Lazy Daisy Spiral

SIZES

Petite (Small, Medium, Large)

MATERIALS

1 1.8oz/10g skein (each approx 37yd/34m) of Creativ Angora (angora) in Lavender

One pair size 7 (4.5mm) needles

One pearl

Tapestry needle

FLOWER

Make a slip knot on LH needle. *Cast on 8 (10, 14, 18) sts, bind off 8 (10, 14, 18) sts, sl LH needle through first cast on st, k and pass rem st on needle over. Sl rem st back on LH needle, do not turn work; rep from * 5 (6, 7, 8) times more. Fasten off.

Run threaded tapestry needle through straight edge of piece, pull tightly and secure. Sew pearl to center.

Lazy Daisy Flat

MATERIALS

1 1¾OZ/50G BALL (EACH APPROX 77YD/72M) OF MUENCH OCEANA (VISCOSE, NYLON, COTTON) IN ASSORTED COLORS

ONE PAIR SIZE 10 (6MM) NEEDLES

TAPESTRY NEEDLE

BEAD FOR CENTER

RHINESTONE FOR CENTER

BEADS FOR HANGING BEAD CENTER

FLOWER

MAKE A SLIP KNOT. *CAST ON 12 STS, BIND OFF 12 STS; SL LH NEEDLE THROUGH FIRST CAST ON ST, K AND PASS REM ST ON NEEDLE OVER IT. SL REM ST BACK ON LH NEEDLE, DO NOT TURN WORK, REP FROM * 6 TIMES MORE. FASTEN OFF.

RUN THREADED TAPESTRY NEEDLE THROUGH STRAIGHT EDGE OF PIECE, PULL TIGHTLY AND SECURE.

CENTER TECHNIQUES

BOBBLE CENTER (SEE PAGE 127). KNOTTED CORD (SEE I-CORD PAGE 127).

CHAPTER FOUR

Felted Stitch Pattern Flowers

Felting flowers is an easy way to become addicted to felting. This technique creates uniquely textured flowers. Any flower can be felted, but natural 100% wool must be used. Superwash wools do not felt. Cashmere and alpaca felt beautifully. Many stitch combinations are used to make the following flowers. A larger gauge than normal is used, making the stitches loose and airy and allowing the soap and hot/cold water to penetrate the wool. This process, along with the agitation, changes the character of the stitches, creating the felted flower.

Trumpet

MATERIALS

1 ⅞oz/25g skein (each approx 82yd/75m) of Jamieson Shetland Double Knitting (pure Shetland wool) in #375 Flax (A)

1 skein each in #791 Pistachio (B) and #1140 Granny Smith (C)

One pair size 8 (5mm) needles

Size 6 (4.25mm) double-pointed needles

Tapestry needle

Beaded fringe (purchased)

FLOWER

With A and size 8 needles, cast on 52 sts.

Row 1 (RS): Purl.

Row 2 K2, *k1, sl this st back to LH needle, lift the next 7 sts on LH needle, 1 at a time, over this st and off needle, [yo] 2 times, k the first st again, k2; rep from *.

Row 3 P1, *p2tog, drop one loop of double [yo] of previous row, [k1f&b] 2 times in rem yo, p1; rep from * to last st, p1—32 sts.

Row 4 Knit.

Row 5 P2tog across row—16 sts.

Rows 6–14 * K1, p1; rep from *.

Row 15 K2 tog across row—8 sts.

Row 16 P2tog across row—4 sts. Cut yarn leaving long tail.

Upon completion of flower, cont with stem as foll: change to dpn and B. K1, k2tog, k1—3 sts. Make cord for desired length. Sew back seam with long tail.

PETALS

With C, make 5 picot chain petals (see pistil flowers, page 102) for each flower. Sew to top of each trumpet where cord begs. Felt (see page 128). Attach beaded fringe to center of flower.

Sunflower

MATERIALS

1 ⅞oz/25g skein (each approx 82yd/75m) of Jamiesons Shetland Double Knitting (pure Shetland wool) in #375 Flax (A)

1 skein each in #425 Mustard (B), #1190 Burnt Umber (C) and #147 Moss (D)

One pair size 8 (5mm) needles

Tapestry needle

MB (Make Bobble)

([K1f&b] 2 times) in same st—4 sts, turn, k 4, turn, p 4, pass 2nd, 3rd, and 4th st over the 1st st—1 st.

Center Bobble Rope

With C, cast on 63 sts

Row 1 (RS) knit.

Row 2 *P3, MB; rep from *, end p3.

Row 3 Bind off all sts pwise. Sew forming a spiral.

INNER CIRCLE OF PETALS

Using 2 strands B, make a slip knot. * Cast on 6 sts, bind off 6 sts; rep from * until 19 petals. Fasten off.

OUTER CIRCLE OF PETALS

Using 2 strands of A, make a slip knot. *Cast on 9 sts, bind off 9 sts; rep from * until 23 petals. Fasten off.

Forming circles, sew inner circle around center; then sew outer circle under inner circle. Felt (see page 128).

LEAF

With D, make 3 large basic leaves (see page 127) and felt (see page 128). Attach to flower.

Five-Star Flower

MATERIALS

1 ⅞oz/25g skein (each approx 82yd/75m) of Jamieson Shetland Double Knitting (pure Shetland wool) in #410 Cornfield (A)

1 skein each #575 Lipstick (B), #600 Violet (C), #232 Blue Lovat (D), #580 Cherry (E) and #791 Olive (F) for leaves

One pair size 8 (5mm) needles

Tapestry needle

LARGE STAR

Using 2 colors for each of the 3 flowers, with 1st color, cast on 6 sts.

Row 1 (RS) K3, yo, k3—7 sts

Rows 2, 4, 6, 8, and 10 Knit.

Row 3 K3, yo, k4—8 sts.

Row 5 K3, yo, k5—9 sts.

Row 7 K3, yo, k6—10 sts.

Row 9 K3, yo, k7—11 sts.

Row 11 K3, yo, k8—12 sts.

Row 12 Bind off 6 sts, k to end—6 sts rem.

Rep rows 1—12 four times more. Bind off.

Sew cast on to bind off edge. Sew to form star. Weave yarn in and out of eyelet, pull tightly and secure.

SMALL STAR

Using 2 colors for each of the 3 flowers, with 1st color, cast on 4 sts.

Row 1 (RS) K2, yo, k2—5 sts.

Rows 2, 4 and 6 Knit.

Row 3 K2, yo, k3—6 sts.

Row 5 K2, yo, k4—7 sts.

Row 7 K2, yo, k5—8 sts.

Row 8 Bind off 4 sts, k to end—4 sts rem.

Rep Rows 1—8 four times more. Bind off.

Sew cast on to bind off edge. Sew to form star. Weave yarn in and out of eyelet, pull tightly and secure.

CENTER

With 2nd color make slip knot. *Cast on 4 sts, bind off 4 sts; rep from * until there are 5 spokes. Run threaded needle through bottom, pull tightly and secure.

Layer small star over larger star and tie center piece in center of star.

Felt flower (see page 128).

LEAF

With F, make 2 small basic leaves (see page 127) for each flower. Felt and attach to flowers.

Florals

COMPONENTS—PISTIL AND BOBBLE

MATERIALS

Small amount ⅞oz/25g skein (each approx 82yd/75m) of Jamieson Double Knitting (pure Shetland wool) in #540 Coral (A)

Small amount in #769 Willow (B)

One pair size 8 (5mm) needles

Tapestry needle

PISTIL With A, make a slip knot. *Cast on 5 sts, bind off 5 sts, sl 1 p st to LH needle; rep from * 6 times more.

BOBBLE With given color, CO 1 st.

Row 1 (K1f&b) 2 times, then k into front once more—5 sts.

Rows 2 and 4 Purl.

Rows 3 and 5 Knit.

Bind off.

Run threaded needle through bottom, pull tightly and secure. With B, make bobble and sew to center flower. Felt (see page 128).

SMALL PETAL, LARGE PETAL AND PISTIL FLOWER

MATERIALS

1 ⅞oz/25g skein (each approx 82yd/75m) of Jamieson Shetland Double Knitting (pure Shetland wool) in #526 Spice (A)

1 skein each in #540 Coral (B), #587 Madder (C) and #769 Willow (D)

One pair size 7 (4.5mm) knitting needles

Tapestry needle

SMALL PETAL

(make 6 petals)

With B, cast on 3 sts. K 1 row. P 1 row. Work in St st inc 1 st each end of needle every other row until there are 5 sts. Work even for 4 rows, ending with a WS row.

NEXT ROW (RS) Ssk, k1, k2tog—3 sts.

NEXT ROW Purl

NEXT ROW Sk2p—1 st. Fasten off.

With A, make 6 bobbles (see page 102) and 1 pistil (see page 102) with 7 spokes. With D, make 3 bobbles. Sew 1 A bobble to end of each of 6 petals. Sew 3 D bobbles to center. Sew pistil around bobbles. Felt (see page 128).

Large Petal

(MAKE 6 PETALS)

WITH A, CAST ON 3 STS. K 1 ROW.
P 1 ROW. WORK IN ST ST INC 1 ST
EACH END OF NEEDLE EVERY
OTHER ROW UNTIL THERE ARE 7
STS. WORK EVEN FOR 5 ROWS,
ENDING WITH A WS ROW.

Row 1 (RS) SSK, K TO LAST 2
STS, K2TOG—2 STS DECREASED.
ROW 2 PURL.
REP ROWS 1 AND 2 UNTIL 3 STS
REM.

Next Row (RS) SK2P—1 ST.
FASTEN OFF.

WITH B, MAKE 6 BOBBLES (SEE
PAGE 102). WITH C, MAKE 1 BOB-
BLE. WITH D, MAKE PISTIL (SEE
PAGE 102) WITH 15 SPOKES. SEW
6 B BOBBLES TO CENTER OF
PETALS. SEW PISTIL TO CENTER
OF LARGE PETALS AROUND BOB-
BLE. SEW C BOBBLE TO CENTER
OF FLOWER. FELT (SEE PAGE
128).

Pistil Flower

WITH A, MAKE 1 PISTIL (SEE PAGE
102) WITH 15 SPOKES. WITH B,
MAKE 1 PISTIL WITH 7 SPOKES.
WITH D, MAKE 1 BOBBLE (SEE
PAGE 102). LAYER B PISTIL OVER
A PISTIL AND SEW TOG WITH D
BOBBLE IN CENTER. FELT (SEE
PAGE 128).

Moody Blue

FELTED AND NOT FELTED

MATERIALS

Small amount ⅞oz/25g skein (each approx 82yd/75m) of Jamieson's Double Knitting 100% Shetland (pure Shetland wool) in #425 Mustard (A)

1 skein each #684 Cobalt (B), #660 Lagoon (C) and #764 Cloud (D)

One pair size 6 (4mm) needles for unfelted version

One pair size 9 (5.5mm) needles for felted version

Tapestry needle

NOTE Use size 6 needles for unfelted version; size 9 needles for felted version.

FLOWER
LARGE PETAL

(make 6)

With B and size 6 or 9 needles (see note), cast on 3 sts. Work in St st, inc 1 st each end every RS row until there are 7 sts. Work even for 4 rows, ending with a WS row.

Row 1 (RS) Ssk, k to last 2 sts, k2tog—5 sts.

Row 2 Purl.

Rep rows 1 and 2 until 3 sts rem. Sk2p—1 st. Fasten off.

SMALL PETAL

(make 6)

With C and size 6 or 9 needles (see note), cast on 3 sts. Work in St st, inc 1 st each end every other row until there are 5 sts. Work even for 4 rows, ending with a WS row.

Rep rows 1 and 2 of large petals until 3 sts rem. Sk2p—1 st. Fasten off.

FLOWER CENTER

With D and size 6 or 9 needles (see note), make a slip knot. *Cast on 5 sts, bind off 5 sts, sl 1 p st to LH needle; rep from * 6 times more. Run thread needle through bottom. Pull tightly and secure.

Felt (see page 128) pieces of felted version. Sew to flower center. Sew large petals to background. Thread cast-on edge sts of small petals, gather and pull tog. Sew to center of large petals.

With A and tapestry needle, make 6 French knots (see page 127) in flower center. Felt (see page 128), if desired.

A Flower on Shoes

MATERIALS

SMALL AMOUNT 1¾OZ/50G SKEIN (EACH APPROX 143YD/130M) SKACEL KARAT (RAYON METALLIC/POLYESTER) IN #02 GOLD

ONE PAIR SIZE 3 (3.25MM) NEEDLES

TAPESTRY NEEDLE

PURCHASED GOLD METALLIC SHOES

NOTE USE CORRESPONDING YARN TO MATCH YOUR CHOICE OF SHOES

PISTIL FLOWER/SMALL BOBBLE
(MAKE 2)

FLOWER MAKE A SLIP KNOT. *CAST ON 5 STS, BIND OFF 5 STS; REP FORM * 8 TIMES MORE. RUN THREAD THROUGH SOLID EDGE. PULL TIGHTLY AND SECURE.

BOBBLE CAST ON 1 ST. K1F&B UNTIL 3 STS. P 1 ROW, K 1 ROW, P 1 ROW. SK2P—1 ST. FASTEN OFF. TIE TO CENTER OF FLOWER.

ATTACH FLOWER AND BOBBLE TO SHOE EITHER BY SEWING OR GLUING TO CENTER OF SHOE.

A Felted Rose Bag

KNITTED MEASUREMENTS

Before felting approx 18"/45.5cm high and 22"/56cm wide at top and 13½"/34cm wide at bottom
After felting approx 13"/33cm high and 16"/40.4cm wide at top and 11"/28cm wide at bottom

MATERIALS

Four 3½oz/100g balls (each approx 60yd/54m) of Tahki Yarns/Tahki•Stacy Charles Inc. Baby (wool) in #22 olive (A)
6 balls in #16 black (B)
4 balls in #32 red (C)
1 ball in #14 dark olive (D)
One pair size 19 (15mm) needles
Tapestry needle

GAUGE

10 sts and 12 rows = 4"/10cm over pat st using size 19 (25mm) needles.
TAKE TIME TO CHECK GAUGE.

PHOTO: PAUL AMATO

TRELLIS PATTERN

(MULTIPLE OF 8 STS PLUS 1)
PREPARATION ROW (WS) WITH A,
P1, *P1 WRAPPING YARN TWICE, P5,
P1 WRAPPING YARN TWICE, P1; REP
FROM * TO END.

ROW 1 WITH B, K1 *SL 1 WYIB
DROPPING EXTRA WRAP, K5, SL 1
WYIB DROPPING EXTRA WRAP, K1;
REP FROM * TO END.

ROW 2 WITH B, P1, *SL 1 WYIF,
P5, SL 1 WYIF, P1; REP FROM * TO
END.

ROW 3 WITH B, K1 *SL 1 WYIB,
K5, SL 1 WYIB, K1; REP FROM * TO
END.

ROW 4 WITH B, P, DROPPING ALL
ELONGATED COLOR A SL STS OFF
NEEDLE TO BACK (I.E. TO RIGHT
SIDE OF FABRIC).

ROW 5 WITH A, K1, SL 1 WYIB, K1,
*PICK UP FIRST DROPPED ST AND
KNIT IT, K1, PICK UP NEXT DROPPED
ST AND KNIT IT; THEN (WITH YARN
IN BACK SL THE LAST 3 STS
WORKED BACK TO LEFT HAND NEE-
DLE, PASS YARN TO FRONT, SL THE
SAME 3 STS BACK AGAIN TO RIGHT
HAND NEEDLE, PASS YARN TO BACK)
TWICE; K 1, SL 3 WYIB, K1; REP
FROM *, END LAST REP SL 1 WYIB,
K1 INSTEAD OF SL 3 WYIB, K1.

ROW 6 WITH A, P 1, SL 1 WYIF,
*[P1, P1 WRAPPING YARN TWICE]
TWICE, P 1, SL 3 WYIF; REP FROM *,
END LAST REP SL 1 WYIF, P 1
INSTEAD OF SL 3 WYIF.

ROW 7 WITH B, K3, *SL 1 WYIB
DROPPING EXTRA WRAP, K1, SL 1
WYIB DROPPING EXTRA WRAP, K 5;
REP FROM * END LAST REP K3.

ROW 8 WITH B, P3, *SL 1 WYIF, P1,
SL 1 WYIF, P 5; REPEAT FROM *,
END LAST REP P3.

ROW 9 WITH B, K3, *SL 1 WYIB,
K1, SL 1 WYIB, K 5; REP FROM *,
END LAST REP K3.

ROW 10 WITH B, PURL, DROPPING
ALL ELONGATED COLOR A SL STS
OFF NEEDLE TO BACK.

ROW 11 WITH A, K1, PICK UP
FIRST DROPPED ST AND KNIT IT, K1,
SL 3 WYIF, K1; REP FROM * OF ROW
5, END PICK UP LAST DROPPED ST
AND KNIT IT, K1.

ROW 12 WITH A, P1, *P1 WRAP-
PING YARN TWICE, P1, SL 3 WYIF,
P1, P1 WRAPPING YARN TWICE, P1;
REP FROM * TO END.

REP ROWS 1-12 FOR TRELLIS PAT.

ROSE

(OVER AN ODD NUMBER OF STS)
CAST ON 15 LEAVING A LONG TAIL
FOR SEAMING.

ROW 1 K1, *P1, K1; REP FROM *
TO END.

ROWS 2, 4, 6 AND 8 K THE KNIT
STS AND P THE PURL STS.

ROW 3 K1, *P1, M1 P-ST, K1; REP
FROM * TO END—22 STS.

ROW 5 K1, *P2, M1 P-ST, K1; REP
FROM *TO END—29 STS.

ROW 7 K1, *P3, M1 P-ST, K1; REP
FROM * TO END—36 STS

BIND OFF ALL STS. ROLL THE RUF-
FLE EDGE AND SEAM TO CAST ON
EDGE TO FORM A ROSE SHAPE.

LEAF

CAST ON 5 STS
ROW 1 (RS) K2, YO, K1, YO, K2—
7 STS.
ROWS 2, 4 AND 6 PURL.

Row 3 Ssk, k 3, k 2 tog—5 sts.
Row 5 Ssk, k1, k 2 tog—3 sts.
Row 7 Sl 1, k 2 tog, psso—1 st.
Fasten off

Front
Note Bag is worked from top down.
With A, cast on 50 sts and work St st for 2"/5cm, end with a WS row. P next row on RS for turning ridge. Cont in St st for 1"/2.5cm more. K next row on RS, inc 15 sts evenly spaced across—65 sts. P 1 row, k 1 row. Work in trellis pat for one full rep. Cont in pat, dec 1 st each side on next row, then every 6th row twice more, then [every other row twice, every 4th row twice] twice, every other row twice. Work even through row 11 of 5th pat rep. With A, p 1 row, k1 row. Bind off.

Back
Work same as front.

Bottom
With B, cast on 10 sts. Work in St st, inc 1 st each side every other row twice—14 sts. Work even for 12"/30.5cm. Dec 1 st each side every other row twice. Bind off.

Handles
(make 2)
With B, cast on 8 sts. Work St st for 22"/56cm. Bind off. Sew seam lengthwise. Piece will form a tube when felted.

Roses
(make 12)
With C, foll rose pattern.

Leaves
(make 21 with A and 12 with D)

Pocket
With B, cast on 12 sts and work St st for 6"/15.5cm. Bind off.

Finishing
Sew side seams of front and back tog. Fold and sew hem to inside. Sew pocket to inside at top under hem. Pin and sew bottom to front and back. Sew handles 6"/15.5cm in from each side edge.

Felting
Note Bag, roses and leaves are felted separately.
Felt pieces (see page 128). After one cycle, check measurements of bag. If it's still larger than finished measurements, repeat process with progressively shorter cycles, measuring every few minutes until measurement is achieved. Form bag into shape. Let air dry.
When felting is complete sew 1 each of A & B leaves to each rose. Sew roses around top edges. Divide and sew remaining leaves to bag front and back. (follow photo)

CHAPTER FIVE

Felted Cut Flowers

Unlike all the flowers in the previous chapters that are made by actually knitting the shapes of the flowers, these flowers are cut from a solid knit fabric that has been felted. By using a template you cut the shape of the petals and sew them together with needle and thread. They can be beautifully adorned with rhinestones, beads, or any other creative touch you might have. They make gorgeous brooches, corsages or stemmed flowers to put in a vase.

Felted Trio

DAHLIA, NEMOROSA, JENNI BLOOM

MATERIALS

DAHLIA (FRONT)

1 1¾OZ/50G SKEIN (EACH APPROX 110YD/104M) OF TRENDSETTER KASHMIR (CASHMERE/SILK) IN #26809 PLUM (A)

SMALL AMOUNT EACH IN #27043 GRAPE (B) AND #25761 FOREST (C)

ONE PAIR SIZE 11 (8MM) NEEDLES OR SIZE TO OBTAIN GAUGE FOR ALL FLOWERS

TAPESTRY NEEDLE

L'ORNA WAND

NEMOROSA (BACK)

1 SKEIN IN #27043 GRAPE (A)

1 SKEIN IN #27018 LIME (B)

CRYSTAL RHINESTONES—42

PINK SEED BEADS—L PACKAGE

JENNI BLOOM (RIGHT)

1 SKEIN IN #27043 GRAPE (A)

1 SKEIN IN #27018 LIME (B)

PINK STUDS—30

GAUGE

7 STS = 2"/5CM BEFORE FELTING. TAKE TIME TO CHECK GAUGE.

Dahlia

With A, cast on 50 sts. Work in
St st until piece measures
10"/25.5cm. Bind off.
With B, cast on 26 sts. Work
in St st until piece measures
1½"/4cm. Bind off.
With C, cast on 28 sts. Work in
St st for 3½"/9cm. Bind off.

Felt pieces (see page 128).
Using templates (see page 130),
cut 14 petals from color A
felted piece. Sew 7 petals at
center for bottom layer, 7 for
top layer. Place top layer on
bottom so petals alternate.
From color B felted piece, cut
a piece 6" x 1"/15 x 2.5cm for
center. Make ½"/1.25cm cuts
across top every ¼"/63cm. Roll
to form spiral and sew to center of petals.
Using jagged leaf template
(see page 130), cut 4 leaves
from felted piece C and attach
to flower.

Nemorosa

With A, cast on 35 sts. Work in
St st for 3"/7.5cm. Bind off.
With B, cast on 16 sts. Work in
St st for 3"/7.5cm. Bind off.

Felt pieces (see page 128).
Using template (see page 130),
cut 6 petals from color A felted piece. Sew petals tog at center. Using L'Orna Wand, glue 7
rhinestones to each petal.
Thread seed beads approx
¾"/2cm length, make

12 lengths sewing each one to center of flower. Using leaf template (see page 130), cut 2 leaves from color B felted piece and sew to flower. Cut 2 circles from color A felted piece and sew one to center front of flower (also one to back of flower for reinforcement, if making a pin).

Jenni Bloom

With A, cast on 30 sts. Work in St st for 2"/5cm. Bind off. With B, cast on 10 sts. Work in St st for 2"/5cm. Bind off.

Felt pieces (see page 128). Using template (see page 130), cut 5 petals from color A felted piece and sew tog at center.

Using L'Orna Wand, glue 6 studs down center of each petal. Using leaf template, cut 3 leaves from color B felted piece, sew to flower. Cut 2 circles from color A felted piece. Sew one to top of flower (also one to bottom for reinforcement, if making a pin).

Hat / Dahlia

MATERIALS

2 1¾ oz/50g skein (each approx 110yd/104m) of Trendsetter Kashmir (cashmere/silk) in #26809 Plum (A)

Small amount in #27043 Grape B (for band)

Small amount in #25761 Forest (C)

One pair size 11 (8mm) needles or size to obtain gauge for all flowers

Tapestry needle

L'Orna Wand

FLOWER AND LEAVES

Make 1 dahlia and 3 jagged leaves (page 118).

HAT

With A, cast on 100 sts. Next **Row (RS)** K, inc 20 sts evenly across row—120 sts. Cont in St st for 5½"/14cm, ending with a WS row.

Next Row (RS) K, dec 20 sts evenly across row—100 sts. Cont in St st for 5½"/14.5cm, ending with a WS row.

CROWN SHAPING

Row 1 *Sk2p, k17; rep from * across—90 sts.

Row 2 and all WS row Purl.

Row 3 *Sk2p, k15; rep from *across—80 sts.

Row 5 *Sk2p, k13; rep from * across—70 sts.

Row 7 *Sk2p, k11; rep from * across—60 sts.

Row 9 *Sk2p, k9; rep from * across—50 sts.

Row 11 *Sk2p, k7; rep from * across—40 sts.

Row 13 *Sk2p, k5; rep from * across—30 sts.

Row 15 *Sk2p, k3; rep from * across—20 sts.

Row 17 *Sk2p, k1; rep from * across—10 sts.

Run threaded tapestry needle through rem sts on needle. Gather up and fasten securely.

BAND

With B, cast on 120 sts. Work St st for 1"/2.5cm. Bind off.

FINISHING

Sew hat seam. Felt hat and band to size (see page 128). Cut band to fit hat circumference at crown, if necessary, and sew to hat. Felt flower and leaves (see page 128) and sew to hat.

Three-Petal Flower

SIZE APPROX 6"/15CM.

MATERIALS

1 1¾OZ/50G BALL (EACH APPROX 220YD/200M) OF NASHUA HAND-KNITS/WESTMINSTER FIBERS (ALPACA/WOOL) IN #0100 NATURAL (A)

1 BALL EACH IN #2380 OATMEAL (B) AND #3249 CHOCOLATE (C)

ONE PAIR SIZE 10 (6MM) NEEDLES

TAPESTRY NEEDLE

ONE GOLD BUTTON

CORRESPONDING COLOR SEWING THREAD

MULTI BROWN FEATHERS (OPTIONAL)—THE BAG SMITH, WWW.THE-BAGSMITH.COM

LARGE PETAL PIECE

(MAKE 1 WITH C AND 1 WITH B)
CAST ON 60 STS. WORK ST ST FOR 46 ROWS. BIND OFF.

SMALL PETAL PIECE

(MAKE 1 WITH A)
CAST ON 40 STS. WORK IN ST ST FOR 25 ROWS. BIND OFF.

FELT (SEE PAGE 128) ALL 3 PIECES. USING PETAL TEMPLATES (SEE PAGE 129), CUT 7 LARGE PETALS FROM C, 7 MEDIUM PETALS FROM B AND 7 SMALL PETALS FROM A. SEW EACH SET OF PETALS TOG TO FORM FLOWER. LAYER DARK TO LIGHT AND SEW TOG. SEW GOLD BUTTON IN CENTER. CUT CIRCLE FROM C AND SEW TO BACK FOR REINFORCEMENT. FEATHERS OPTIONAL (SEE PHOTO).

Angel Rose

MATERIALS

1 1¾oz/50g ball (each approx 220yd/207m) of Nashua hand-knits/Westminster Fibers (alpaca/wool) in #0100 Natural (A)

1 ball each in #1837 Soft Pink (B), #2540 Ciel (C) and #1256 Soft Sage (D)

One pair size 10 (6mm) needles

Tapestry needle

ROSE

(make 1 each in A, B and C)

Cast on 60 sts. Work in St st for 50 rows. Bind off.

Felt pieces (see page 128).

LEAF

With D, cast on 40 sts. Work in St st for 30 rows. Bind off. Felt piece (see page 128).

Using templates (see page 129), cut 4 petals and 1 center piece for each rose. Form spiral beg with short side in, stitch in place. Fold and stitch each petal at bottom center. Sew 4 petals around center. Using template, cut 2 larger and 1 small leaf for each flower. Sew to flowers.

ABBREVIATIONS

APPROX APPROXIMATELY

BEG BEGIN(NING)

BIND OFF USED TO FINISH AN EDGE AND KEEP STITCHES FROM UNRAVELING. LIFT THE FIRST STITCH OVER THE SECOND, THE SECOND OVER THE THIRD, ETC.

CO (CAST ON) A FOUNDATION ROW OF STITCHES PLACED ON THE NEEDLE IN ORDER TO BEGIN KNITTING.

CC CONTRAST COLOR

CONT CONTINUE(ING)

DEC DECREASE(ING)—REDUCE THE STITCHES IN A ROW (KNIT 2 TOGETHER).

DPN DOUBLE-POINTED NEEDLE(S)

FOLL FOLLOW(S)(ING)

G GRAM(S)

GARTER STITCH KNIT EVERY ROW. CIRCULAR KNITTING: KNIT ONE ROUND, THEN PURL ONE ROUND.

INC INCREASE(ING)—ADD STITCHES IN A ROW (KNIT INTO THE FRONT AND BACK OF A STITCH)

K KNIT

K2TOG KNIT 2 STITCHES TOGETHER

LH LEFT-HAND

LP(S) LOOP(S)

M METER(S)

M1 MAKE ONE STITCH—WITH THE NEEDLE TIP, LIFT THE STRAND BETWEEN LAST STITCH WORKED AND NEXT STITCH ON THE LEFT-HAND NEEDLE AND KNIT INTO THE BACK OF IT. ONE KNIT STITCH HAS BEEN ADDED.

M1-P MAKE ONE PURL STITCH—WITH THE NEEDLE TIP, LIFT THE STRAND BETWEEN LAST STITCH WORKED AND NEXT STITCH ON THE LEFT-HAND NEEDLE AND PURL INTO THE BACK OF IT. ONE PURL STITCH HAS BEEN ADDED.

MC MAIN COLOR

MM MILLIMETER(S)

OZ OUNCE(S)

P PURL

P2TOG PURL 2 STITCHES TOGETHER

PAT PATTERN

PICK UP AND KNIT (PURL) KNIT (OR PURL) INTO THE LOOPS ALONG AN EDGE.

PM PLACE MARKERS—PLACE OR ATTACH A LOOP OF CONTRASTING YARN OR PURCHASED STITCH MARKER AS INDICATED.

PSSO PASS SLIP STITCH(ES) OVER

REM REMAIN(S)(ING)

REP REPEAT

REV St St REVERSE STOCKINETTE STITCH—PURL RIGHT-SIDE ROWS, KNIT WRONG-SIDE ROWS. CIRCULAR KNITTING: PURL ALL ROUNDS.

RND(S) ROUND(S)

RH RIGHT-HAND

RS RIGHT SIDE(S)

S2KP SLIP 2 STITCHES, KNIT 1, PASS THE 2 SLIPPED STITCHES OVER THE KNIT 1.

SK SKIP

SKP SLIP 1, KNIT 1, PASS SLIP STITCH OVER THE KNIT 1.

SK2P SLIP 1, KNIT 2 TOGETHER, PASS SLIP STITCH OVER THE KNIT 2 TOGETHER.

SL SLIP—AN UNWORKED STITCH MADE BY PASSING A STITCH FROM THE LEFT-HAND TO THE RIGHT-HAND NEEDLE AS IF TO PURL.

SL ST SLIP STITCH

SSK SLIP, SLIP, KNIT—SLIP NEXT 2 STITCHES KNITWISE, ONE AT A TIME, TO RIGHT-HAND NEEDLE. INSERT TIP OF LEFT-HAND NEEDLE INTO FRONTS OF THESE STITCHES FROM LEFT TO RIGHT. KNIT THEM TOGETHER. ONE STITCH HAS BEEN DECREASED.

SSSK SLIP NEXT 3 STS KNITWISE, ONE AT A TIME, TO RIGHT-HAND NEEDLE. INSERT TIP OF LEFT-HAND NEEDLE INTO FRONTS OF THESE STITCHES FROM LEFT TO RIGHT. KNIT THEM TOGETHER. TWO STITCHES HAVE BEEN DECREASED.

ST(S) STITCH(ES)

St St STOCKINETTE STITCH—KNIT RIGHT-SIDE ROWS, PURL WRONG-SIDE ROWS. CIRCULAR KNITTING: KNIT ALL ROUNDS.

TBL THROUGH BACK OF LOOP

TOG TOGETHER

WS WRONG SIDE(S)

WYIB WITH YARN IN BACK

WYIF WITH YARN IN FRONT

WORK EVEN CONTINUE IN PATTERN WITHOUT INCREASING OR DECREASING.

YD YARD(S)

YO YARN OVER—MAKE A NEW STITCH BY WRAPPING THE YARN OVER THE RIGHT-HAND NEEDLE.

***** = REPEAT DIRECTIONS FOLLOWING * AS MANY TIMES AS INDICATED.

[ ] = REPEAT DIRECTIONS INSIDE BRACKETS AS MANY TIMES AS INDICATED.

TECHNIQUES

BASIC LEAF CLASSICS (SMALL AND LARGE)

SMALL

CAST ON 5 STS.

ROW 1 (RS) K2, YO, K1, YO, K2—7 STS.

ROWS 2, 4 AND 6 P.

ROW 3 SSK, K3, K2TOG—5 STS.

ROW 5 SSK, K1 K2TOG—3 STS.

ROW 7 SK2P—1 ST. FASTEN OFF.

LARGE

CAST ON 5 STS.

ROW 1 (RS) K2, YO, K1, YO, K 2—7 STS.

ROW 2 AND ALL EVEN-NUMBERED ROWS P.

ROW 3 K3, YO, K1, YO, K3—9 STS.

ROW 5 K4, YO, K 1, YO, K4—11 STS.

ROW 7 SSK, K7, K2TOG—9 STS.

ROW 9 SSK, K5, K2TOG—7 STS.

ROW 11 SSK, K3, K2TOG—5 STS.

ROW 13 SSK, K1, K2TOG—3 STS.

ROW 15 SK2P—1 ST. FASTEN OFF.

GARTER LEAVES (3 SIZES)

PETITE LEAF

CAST ON 9 STS.

ROWS 1 AND 3 K3, S2KP, K3—7 STS.

ROWS 2 AND 4 K1, M1, K2, P1, K2, M1, K1—9 STS.

ROW 4 K3, P1, K3.

ROW 5 K2, S2KP, K2—5 STS.

ROW 6 K2, P1, K2.

ROW 7 K1, S2KP, K1—3 STS.

ROW 8 K1, P1, K1.

ROW 9 S2KP—1 ST. FASTEN OFF.

SMALL

CAST ON 9 STS.

ROWS 1, 3 AND 5 K3, S2KP, K3—7 STS.

ROWS 2 AND 4 K1, M1, K2, P1, K2, M1, K1—9 STS.

ROW 6 K3, P1, K3.

ROW 7 K1, S2KP, K2—5 STS.

ROW 8 K2, P1, K2.

ROW 9 S2KP, K1—3 STS.

ROW 10 K1, P1, K1.

ROW 11 S2KP—1 ST. FASTEN OFF.

LARGE

CAST ON 15 STS.

ROW 1 K6, S2KP, K 6—13 STS.

ROW 2 K6, P1, K6.

ROW 3 K5, S2KP, K5—11 STS.

ROW 4 K5, P1, K5.

ROW 5 K4, S2KP, K4—9 STS.

ROW 6 K4, P1, K4.

ROW 7 K3, S2KP, K3—7 STS

ROW 8 K3, P1, K3.

ROW 9 K2, S2KP, K2—5 STS.

ROW 10 K2, P1, K2.

ROW 11 K1, S2KP, K1—3 STS

ROW 12 K1, P1, K1.

ROW 13 S2KP—1 ST. FASTEN OFF.

BOBBLE

WITH GIVEN COLOR, MAKE A SLIP KNOT. K INTO FRONT, BACK, FRONT, BACK AND FRONT UNTIL 5 STS ON NEEDLE. TURN. P 1 ROW, K 1 ROW, P 1 ROW.

NEXT ROW K2TOG, K1, K2TOG.

NEXT ROW P3TOG.

DRAW YARN THROUGH REM ST.

FRENCH KNOT

BRING NEEDLE OUT OF CENTER OF FLOWER FROM BACK TO FRONT, WRAP YARN AROUND NEEDLE THREE TIMES AND USE YOUR THUMB TO HOLD IT IN PLACE AS YOU PULL NEEDLE THROUGH THE WRAPS INTO THE CENTER OF THE FLOWER A SHORT DISTANCE (1 BACKGROUND THREAD) FROM WHERE THE THREAD FIRST EMERGED.

I-CORD

CAST ON 3 STS.

ROW 1 K3, DO NOT TURN, SLIDE STS TO OTHER END OF NEEDLE.

REP ROW 1 FOR DESIRED LENGTH. BIND OFF.

TECHNIQUES

FELTING

FILL WASHING MACHINE TO LOW WATER SETTING AT A HOT TEMPERATURE. ADD ¼ CUP OF A GENTLE DETERGENT. ADD ALL PIECES AND A PAIR OF JEANS TO PROVIDE ABRASION AND BALANCED AGITATION. USE 15-20 MINUTE WASH CYCLE, INCLUDING COLD RINSE AND SPIN. CHECK MEASUREMENTS OF PIECE. IF IT IS STILL LARGER THAN FINISHED MEASUREMENTS, REPEAT PROCESS WITH PROGRESSIVELY SHORTER CYCLES, MEASURING EVERY FEW MINUTES UNTIL MEASUREMENT IS ACHIEVED. FORM PIECE INTO SHAPE. LET AIR DRY.

FELTING BY HAND IS MORE LABOR INTENSIVE THAN FELTING BY MACHINE, BUT IT WASTES LESS WATER, PARTICULARLY WHEN YOU ARE FELTING A SWATCH OR A SMALL PROJECT.

SOAK THE FINISHED ITEM IN HOT WATER FOR THIRTY MINUTES OR UNTIL IT IS COMPLETELY SATURATED. ADD A SMALL AMOUNT OF SOAP. AGITATE THE PIECE BY RUBBING AND KNEADING. THIS MAY TAKE SOME TIME, SO BE PATIENT. IF THE WATER COOLS, ADD MORE HOT WATER.

WHEN THE FIBERS ARE MATTED AND YOU DON'T WANT THE ITEM TO SHRINK ANY MORE, RINSE IT IN TEPID WATER. ROLL ITEM IN A TOWEL AND SQUEEZE OUT EXCESS WATER. DO NOT WRING—IT MAY PULL THE ITEM OUT OF SHAPE!

CABLE CAST-ON

1 *INSERT THE RIGHT NEEDLE BETWEEN THE TWO STITCHES ON THE LEFT NEEDLE.

2 WRAP THE YARN AROUND THE RIGHT NEEDLE AS IF TO KNIT AND PULL THE YARN THROUGH TO MAKE A NEW STITCH.

3 PLACE THE NEW STITCH ON THE LEFT NEEDLE AS SHOWN. REPEAT FROM THE *, ALWAYS INSERTING THE RIGHT NEEDLE IN BETWEEN THE LAST TWO STITCHES ON THE LEFT NEEDLE.

TEMPLATES

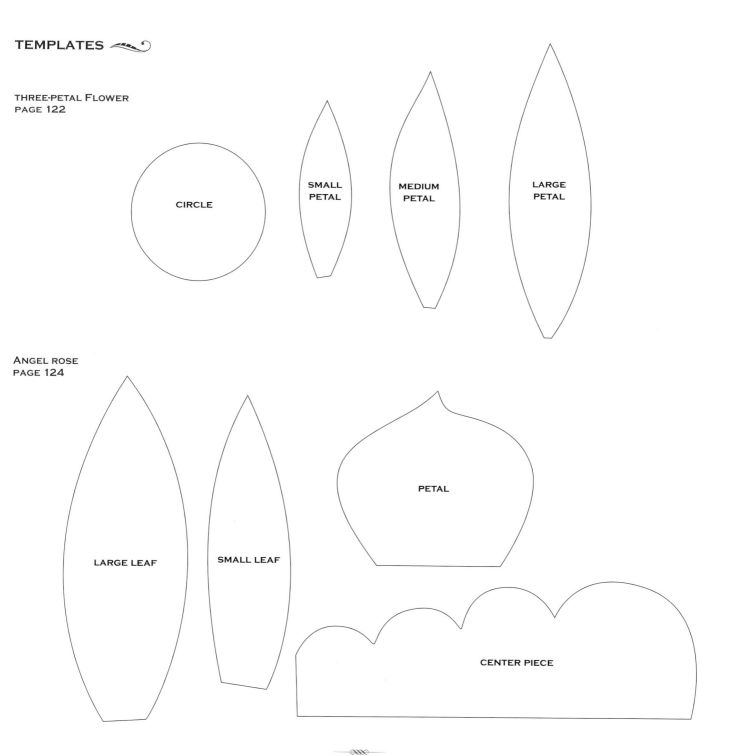

THREE-PETAL FLOWER
PAGE 122

CIRCLE

SMALL
PETAL

MEDIUM
PETAL

LARGE
PETAL

ANGEL ROSE
PAGE 124

LARGE LEAF

SMALL LEAF

PETAL

CENTER PIECE

TEMPLATES

FELTED TRIO
PAGE 118 AND 119

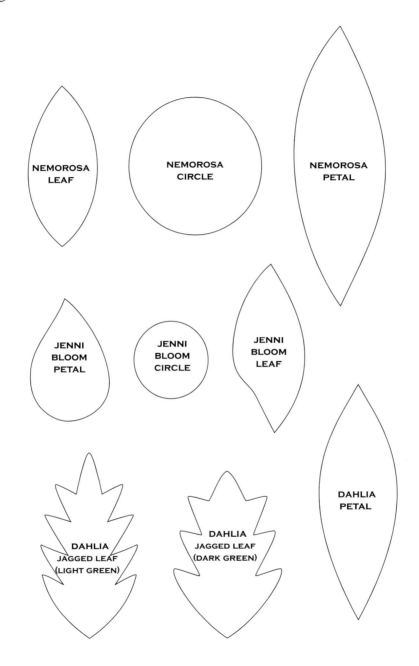

NEMOROSA
LEAF

NEMOROSA
CIRCLE

NEMOROSA
PETAL

JENNI
BLOOM
PETAL

JENNI
BLOOM
CIRCLE

JENNI
BLOOM
LEAF

DAHLIA
JAGGED LEAF
(LIGHT GREEN)

DAHLIA
JAGGED LEAF
(DARK GREEN)

DAHLIA
PETAL

SCHEMATICS

CARDI WRAP
PAGE 38

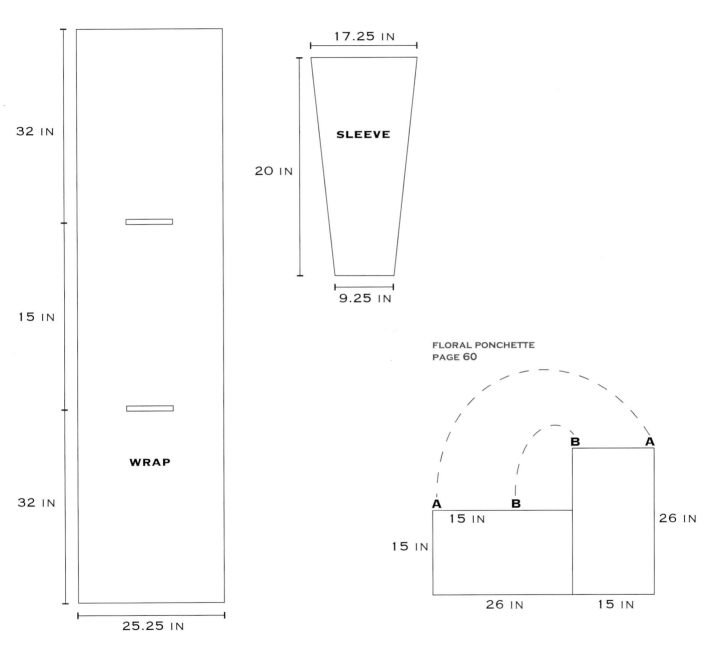

SLEEVE

17.25 IN

20 IN

9.25 IN

WRAP

32 IN

15 IN

32 IN

25.25 IN

FLORAL PONCHETTE
PAGE 60

B   A

A   B

15 IN

15 IN

26 IN

26 IN   15 IN

RESORCES

ALCHEMY YARNS
P.O. Box 1080
Sebastopol, CA 95473
www.alchemyyarns.com

ANNY BLATT / BOUTON D' OR
7796 Boardwalk
Brighton, MI 48116
www.annyblatt.com

BERROCO, INC.
14 Elmdale Road
P.O. Box 367
Uxbridge, MA 01569
In Canada:
Distributed by
S.R. Kertzer, Ltd.
www.berroco.com

BLUE SKY ALPACAS
P.O. Box 387
St. Francis, MN 55070
www.blueskyalpacas.com

CLASSIC ELITE YARNS
122 Western Avenue
Lowell, MA 01851
www.classiceliteyarns.com

DIAMOND YARN
9697 St. Laurent
Montreal, Quebec PQ H3L 2N1
and 155 Martin Ross, Unit #3
Toronto, ON M3J 2L9
www.diamondyarn.com

FILATURA DI CROSA
Distributed by
Tahki•Stacy Charles, Inc.
In Canada:
Distributed by Diamond Yarn
www.tahkistacycharles.com

JCA, INC.
35 Scales Lane
Townsend, MA 01469
www.jcacrafts.com

KARABELLA YARNS, INC.
1201 Broadway, Suite 311
New York, NY 10001
www.karabellayarns.com

KNIT ONE CROCHET TOO
91 Tandberg Trail, Unit 6
Windham, ME 04062
www.knitonecrochettoo.com

KOIGU WOOL DESIGNS
RR #1
Williamsford, ON N0H 2V0
Canada
www.koigu.com

LANA GROSSA
www.lanagrossa.de
Distributed by
Unicorn Books and Crafts
www.unicornbooks.com

LION BRAND YARN
34 West 15th Street
New York, NY 10011
www.lionbrand.com
In Canada:
Distributed by
Domcord Belding
660 Denison St.
Markham, ON L3R 1C1

MUENCH YARNS
1323 Scott Street
Petaluma, CA 94954
In Canada:
Distributed by
Les Fils Muench
5640 Rue Valcourt
Brossard, Quebec J4W 1C5
www.myyarns.com

NASHUA HANDKNITS
Distributed by
Westminister Fibers
4 Townsend West, Unit 8
Nashua, NH 03063

PLYMOUTH YARN
P.O. Box 28
Bristol, PA 19007
www.plymouthyarn.com

PRISM
3140 39th Ave. North
St. Peterburg, FL 33714
www.prismyarn.com

ROWAN YARNS
Distributed by
Westminister Fibers
www.westministerfibers.com
4 Townsend West, Unit 8
Nashua, NH 03063
www.knitrowan.com

SIMPLY SHETLAND
P.O. Box 751264
Petaluma, CA 94975
www.simplyshetland.net

SKACEL COLLECTION
8041 South 180th Street
Kent, WA 98032
www.skacelknitting.com

TAHKI•STACY CHARLES, INC.
70-30 80th Street
Building #36
Ridgewood, NY 11385
www.tahkistacycharles.com

TRENDSETTER YARNS
16745 Saticoy Street, #101
Van Nuys, CA 91406
www.trendsetteryarns.com

UNICORN BOOKS &
CRAFTS, INC.
1338 Ross Street
Petaluma, CA 94954
www.unicornbooks.com

Acknowledgments

ONE OF THE PLEASURES OF WRITING THIS BOOK WAS THE WONDERFUL
PEOPLE I WAS ABLE TO WORK WITH. I WAS HELPED BY THE SOHO STAFF, WHO
KEPT THE ORGANIZATION AND PRODUCTION ON TRACK. SO, A DOZEN ROSES FOR
TRISHA MALCOLM, CARLA SCOTT, ERICA SMITH, LILLIAN ESPOSITO, RACHEL
STEIN AND VERONICA MANNO. AND A SPECIAL BOUQUET FOR CHI LING MOY, MY
FABULOUS ART DIRECTOR, AND TO JENNIFER LEVY AND TRUDY GIORDANO FOR THE
LOVELY PHOTOGRAPHY. CORSAGES FOR EILEEN CURRY, NANCY HENDERSON AND
HERRIS STENZEL, WHO ARE ALWAYS THERE FOR ME. A WREATH OF GRATITUDE TO
ALL THE YARN COMPANIES WHO GENEROUSLY SUPPLIED YARN FOR THE PROJECT. A
GARDEN OF THANKS TO MY READERS AND STUDENTS—AND FINALLY A POPPY TO MY
HUSBAND, HOWARD, WHO HAS BOUGHT FLOWERS FOR ME FOR MANY YEARS.

INDEX